Counterinsurgency Warfare

COUNTERINSURGENCY WARFARE

Theory and Practice

David Galula

Foreword by John A. Nagl

PSI Classics of the Counterinsurgency Era

Praeger Security International
Westport, Connecticut • London

Library of Congress Cataloging-in-Publication Data

Galula, David, 1919-1967.
    Counterinsurgency warfare : theory and practice / David Galula; Foreword by John A.
Nagl.
        p. cm. — (PSI Classics of the Counterinsurgency Era)
    Includes bibliographical references and index.
    ISBN 0-275-99269-1 (alk. paper) – ISBN 0-275-99303-5 (pbk : alk. paper)
    1. Guerrilla warfare   I. Title   II. Series
U240.G3 1964
355.425   64013387

British Library Cataloguing in Publication Data is available.

Library of Congress Catalog Card Number: 64013387
ISBN: 0–275–99269–1
        0–275–99303–5 (pbk.)

First published in 1964

Praeger Security International, 88 Post Road West, Westport, CT 06881
An imprint of Greenwood Publishing Group, Inc.
www.praeger.com

Printed in the United States of America

The paper used in this book complies with the
Permanent Paper Standard issued by the National
Information Standards Organization (Z39.48–1984).

10   9   8   7   6   5   4   3   2   1

CONTENTS

FOREWORD

The best writings on counterinsurgency share with the best sex manuals the fact that their authors generally have some personal experience of their subject matter. Praeger's companion pieces to this text were written by army officers who knew well the cold, hard facts of counterinsurgency.

David Galula drank as deeply of this bitter draught as did his contemporaries and reflected on it even more profoundly. A Frenchman raised in Casablanca, he was graduated from Saint Cyr in 1939, in time to fight in North Africa, Italy, and France. Later assignments included irregular wars in China, Greece, Indochina, and Algeria. Galula was a lieutenant colonel when he took the opportunity to reflect on his experience and wrote *Counterinsurgency Warfare: Theory and Practice* on a fellowship in the Center for International Affairs at Harvard. He died a few years later, missing the chance to observe the American military ignore most of his prescriptions on Vietnam.

Galula's primacy of place in the canon of irregular warfare is secured by his lucid instructions on how counterinsurgency forces can protect and hence gain support of the populace, acquire information on the identity and location of insurgents, and thereby defeat the insurgency. While the primary challenge of conventional warfare is massing firepower at the appropriate place and time to destroy the enemy, the key to success in counterinsurgency is massing intelligence derived from the local population to identify the enemy; the counterinsurgent is literally dying for that information.

Galula points out a basic difference between conventional war and insurgency. While conventional warfare is largely the same experience for all sides concerned, the contestants in an insurgency fight different wars conducted under different rules. An insurgent force has comparatively few weapons and no army; if it openly appears on the same battlefield as the counterinsurgency force, it will be swiftly defeated. What it does have is political control over at least some of the population and, as a result, a shield from behind which to strike its conventional opponent at will.

An insurgency is a competition between insurgent and government for the support of the civilian population, which provides the sea in which the insurgent swims. Galula reminds us that the "counterinsurgent cannot achieve much if the population is not, and does not feel, protected against the insurgent." An insecure population will not provide the necessary information to the counterinsurgent: "intelligence has to come from the population, but the population will not talk unless it feels safe, and it does not feel safe until the insurgent's power has been broken." If they fear retribution from insurgents, civilians will not cooperate with officials. Government agents, then, must be able to establish sufficient presence in any given locality to separate the insurgents from the civilians they exploit.

This is a painstaking process. First, civilians must be separated from insurgents using road blocks, identity cards, and a census. Next, the counterinsurgent must guarantee civilian security by training local security forces who are then readily available for manning the road blocks and conducting the census. Finally, the government should target the insurgents armed with specific, local information derived from long and close association with the population. Not rocket science—but if it were, western militaries would be better at it. Sadly, the military-industrial complex does not build many tools for fighting counterinsurgencies.

Protecting the population by establishing local security forces is not the same as focusing counterinsurgency forces on killing insurgents. Although protecting the local people clearly requires some kinetic actions against committed insurgents, conventional military forces are too prone to emphasize offensive actions such as capturing or killing terrorists rather than the predominantly political, economic, and security requirements upon which the ultimate defeat of the insurgency depends. Some today would marry the intelligence available from civilians to sophisticated weapons systems to create targeted killing campaigns against insurgent leadership. This approach offers only false hope; for every insurgent captured or killed another one (or often several) will appear—so long as they are enabled by passive civilians and a moribund government presence. To win, the government must secure and control the local population.

Doing so in the media age demands more exacting measures than merely building concentration camps. "Control of the population obviously begins with a census," that according to Galula, "if properly made and exploited, is a basic source of intelligence." The static elements of population control are ultimately more important than clearing the enemy using kinetic raids and sweeps. Those forces embedded with the local population become intelligence collectors and analysts—the keys to ultimate victory. They are the holders and builders, and generally should consist of local forces leavened with advisers from the counterinsurgent force.

> The aim of control is to cut off, or at least reduce significantly, the con-tacts between the population and the guerrillas. This is done by watching the population's activities . . . This process of getting acquainted with the population may be speeded up if the occupied villages are divided into sections and each assigned to a group of soldiers *who will always work there* [emphasis added].

Information gained by these soldiers-in-residence cannot be obtained by satellite imagery or monitoring cell phones. Much of what the counterinsurgent is collecting is not actionable intelligence in the short term, while even specific intelligence regarding insurgent identities and locations will only be provided within the trusting atmosphere of a long-standing relationship. Civilians must believe that the counterinsurgent will be able to protect them from retaliation once such critical information is provided. Technology is no substitute for boots on the ground among the population, and numbers matter—Galula suggests that "a ratio of force of ten or twenty to one between the counterinsurgent and the insurgent is not uncommon." The reason behind the disparity in numbers is simple; "disorder—the normal state of nature—is cheap to create and very costly to prevent." Protecting or rebuilding a state is much harder than toppling its government, demanding a far greater investment of time, treasure, and intellect.

Conventional armies are not well suited to the demands of counterinsurgency. The firepower on which they pride themselves cannot be leveraged against the insurgent; in fact, an almost entirely different orientation is necessary, one in which "a mimeograph machine may turn out to be more useful than a machine gun, a soldier trained as a pediatrician more important than a mortar expert, cement more wanted than barbed wire, clerks more in demand than riflemen." Galula prescribes a lightly armored force equipped with a surplus of interpreters, intelligence analysts, civil affairs specialists, and engineers. Counterinsurgents who cannot or do not communicate with the population are doomed to abject failure.

The control of information is strategically decisive in counterinsurgency. It is the insurgent's primary weapon, while the civilian population is its main target and also the battlefield on which the war is fought. Key terrain in an insurgency is not a physical space, but the political loyalty of the people who inhabit that space. Counterinsurgency is not a fair fight, as "the insurgent, having no responsibility, is free to use every trick if necessary, he can lie, cheat, exaggerate. He is not obligated to prove; he is judged by what he promises, not what he does." It is essential, then, for the counterinsurgent to fight an even more adroit information war; in his chapter on operations, Galula devotes more than three times as much attention to information operations as to traditional kinetic warfare. His clear implication is that conventional forces must reorganize themselves in a similar ratio of information operators (including intelligence collectors as well as disseminators) to be effective in this kind of war.

Modifying organizations, training, and equipment of conventional armed forces, critical as it is, is insufficient to satisfy the demands of counterinsurgency operations. Galula argues that "it is just as important that the minds of the leaders and the men—and this includes the civilian as well as the military—be adapted also to the special demands of counterinsurgency warfare." Not all soldiers can adapt, and putting those who cannot in command of a counterinsurgency effort is counterproductive. "A workable solution," he added, "is to identify those who readily accept the new concepts of counterinsurgency warfare and give them responsibility. Those who then prove themselves in action should be pushed upward."

Soldiers who strove to emulate Napoleon's successes of the 19th and 20th centuries studied the maneuver of large armies on the conventional battlefield and mastered the technology that created industrial and then information-age armies. By their very successes in conventional war, western militaries have driven the enemies of modern civilization to adapt the methods of the insurgent. Those who aspire to high command in the new age of irregular warfare should study cultural anthropology, economics, political science, international relations, and languages in addition to conventional warfare. They must also master the principles of both insurgency and counterinsurgency—and understand the differences between the two forms of warfare.

Today, too many soldiers learn those lessons firsthand in the hard classrooms of insurgencies in deserts, jungles, and cities around the globe. Although Galula's book is short enough to be read in theater between coping with improvised explosive devices and mortar attacks, far better for its lessons to be absorbed in the classrooms of staff colleges and military academies. But wherever it is read in this age of competing and cooperating global, transnational, and regional insurgencies, it is hard to find any book whose lessons can be more profitably learned by those who may follow Galula down the streets without joy of couunterinsurgency—a journey likely to be the fate of many more soldiers in the 21st century than was the case even in the counterinsurgency era of 20th century.

John A. Nagl

May 2006

Lieutenant Colonel John A. Nagl, USA, is a Military Assistant to the Deputy Secretary of Defense and the author of *Learning to Eat Soup with a Knife: Counterinsurgency Lessons from Malaya and Vietnam.*

INTRODUCTION

The laws of war—this is a problem that anyone directing a war must study and solve.

The laws of revolutionary war—this is a problem that anyone directing a revolutionary war must study and solve.

The laws of China's revolutionary war—this is a problem that anyone directing a revolutionary war in China must study and solve.

—MAO TSE-TUNG, *Strategic Problems of China's Revolutionary War* (December, 1936)

No chess player has ever found, nor is any likely to find, a sure way of winning from the first move. The game contains too many variables even for one of today's nerveless electronic computers to plot out a guaranteed checkmate.

War is not a chess game but a vast social phenomenon with an infinitely greater and ever-expanding number of variables, some of which elude analysis. Who can deny the importance of luck in war, for instance, and who can assess luck in advance? When Mussolini precipitated a war in the Balkans, forcing Hitler to waste the best part of the spring of 1941 in a secondary theater and to delay the prepared German attack on Soviet Russia, he may well have saved Moscow. It can be argued that this event involved no element of luck, but rather a flagrant error on the part of the Axis: Mussolini should have consulted his partner. Yet since Stalin had played no part in Mussolini's decision, what conclusion can be reached except that Stalin was extremely lucky?

The profusion of variables in war has never discouraged the search for foolproof systems. Because war can be a matter of life and death to states and nations, few other fields of human activity have been so consistently, thoroughly, and actively analyzed. Ever since men have thought and fought (sometimes in the reverse order), attempts have been made to study war—philosophically, because the human mind loves, and needs to lean on, a frame of reference; practically, with the object of drawing useful lessons for the next war.

Such studies have led, in extreme cases, to the denial that any lesson at all can be inferred from past wars, if it is asserted that the conduct of war is only a matter of inspiration and circumstances; or conversely, they have led to the construction of doctrines and their retention as rigid articles of faith, regardless of facts and situation. French military history offers a remarkable example of oscillation between these two poles. The French had no theory, no plan in the 1870–71 Franco-Prussian War. In 1940, they duplicated a recipe proved during World War I and fought a 1918-type of war against the German panzer divisions. The result in both cases was disastrous.

Nevertheless, from studies and accumulated experience, observations have emerged of certain recurrent facts that have been formulated into "laws" of war. They do not, of course, have the same strict value as laws in physical science. However, they cannot be seriously challenged, if only because they confirm what plain common sense tells us. And they are very few in number. Thus, it is the first law that the strongest camp usually wins; hence Napoleon's axiom, "Victory goes to the large battalion." If the contending camps are equally strong, the more resolute wins; this is the second law. If resolution is equally strong, then victory belongs to the camp that seizes and keeps the initiative—the third law. Surprise, according to the fourth law, may play a decisive role. These laws, substantiated by countless cases, constitute the ABC's of warfare. They have, in turn, begotten guiding principles such as concentration of efforts, economy of forces, freedom of action, safety. Application of these principles may change from epoch to epoch as technology, armament, and other factors change, but they retain in general their value throughout the evolution of warfare.

In most wars, the same laws and principles hold equally true for both contending sides. What varies is the way each opponent uses them, according to his ability, his particular situation, his relative strength. Conventional war belongs to this general case.

Revolutionary war, on the other hand, represents an exceptional case not only because, as we suspect, it has its special rules, different from those of the conventional war, but also because most of the rules applicable to one side do not work for the other. In a fight between a fly and a lion, the fly cannot deliver a knockout blow and the lion cannot fly. It is the same war for both camps in terms of space and time, yet there are two distinct warfares—the revolutionary's and, shall we say, the counterrevolutionary's.

This is where Mao Tse-tung is misleading. What he calls "the laws of revolutionary war" are in fact those of the revolutionary side, his side. The one who directs a war against a revolutionary movement will not find in Mao and in other revolutionary theorists the answers to his problems. He will surely find useful information on how the revolutionary acts, he may perhaps infer the answers he is looking for, but nowhere will he find them explicitly stated. Some counterrevolutionaries have fallen into the trap of aping the revolutionaries on both minor and major scales, as we shall show. These attempts have never met success.

What, then, are the rules of counterrevolutionary warfare? Here we can observe another curious fact. Although analyses of revolutionary wars from the revolutionary's point of view are numerous today, there is a vacuum of studies from the other side, particularly when it comes to suggesting concrete courses of action for the counterrevolutionary. Very little is offered beyond formulas—which are sound enough as far as they go—such as, "Intelligence is the key to the problem," or "The support of the population must be won." How to turn the key, how to win the support, this is where frustrations usually begin, as anyone can testify who, in a humble or in an exalted position, has been involved in a revolutionary war on the wrong—i.e., the arduous—side. The junior officer in the field who, after weeks and months of endless tracking, has at last destroyed the dozen guerrillas opposing him, only to see them replaced by a fresh dozen; the civil servant who pleaded in vain for a five-cent reform and is now ordered to implement at once a hundred-dollar program when he no longer controls the situation in his district; the general who has "cleared" Sector A but screams because "they" want to take away two battalions for Sector B; the official in charge of the press who cannot satisfactorily explain why, after so many decisive victories, the rebels are still vigorous and expanding; the congressman who cannot understand why the government should get more money when it has so little to show for the huge appropriations previously granted; the chief of state, harassed from all sides, who wonders how long he will last—these are typical illustrations of the plight of the counterrevolutionary.

There is clearly a need for a compass, and this work has as its only purpose to construct such an instrument, however imperfect and rudimentary it may be. What we propose to do is to define the laws of counterrevolutionary warfare, to deduce from them its principles, and to outline the corresponding strategy and tactics.

The enterprise is risky. First of all, whereas conventional wars of any size and shape can be counted in the hundreds, no more than a score of revolutionary wars have occurred, most of them since 1945. Is it enough to detect laws? Generalization and extrapolation from such a limited basis must rely to some extent on intuition, which may or may not be correct. Then there is the pitfall of dogmatism inherent in any effort at abstraction, for we are not studying a specific counterrevolutionary war, but the problem in general; what may seem relevant in a majority of cases may not be so in others where particular factors have affected the events in a decisive way.

We shall not claim, therefore, that we are providing the whole and complete answer to the counterrevolutionary's problems. We hope merely to clear away some of the confusions that we have so often and so long witnessed in the "wrong" camp.

What is primarily dealt with here is counterrevolutionary warfare in the areas called "colonial" and "semicolonial" by the Communists, and "underdeveloped" by us. That revolutionary wars can occur outside these areas is possible, but their success would be far from certain, for a stable society is obviously less vulnerable. In recent times, only one revolutionary war has taken place in a "capitalist" area—in Greece in 1945–50—and the revolutionaries were defeated. We may perhaps see the beginning of another in the Quebec Province of Canada today. In any case, we believe that the problem is not acute in the developed parts of the world.

A matter of semantics has to be cleared up before proceeding further. It is unwise to concede to Mao Tse-tung that the revolutionary's opponent is a "counterrevolutionary," for this word has come to be synonymous with "reactionary," which has not always been, nor will it always be, the case. Therefore, one side will be called the "insurgent" and his action the "insurgency"; on the opposite side, we will find the "counterinsurgent" and the "counterinsurgency." Since insurgency and counterinsurgency are two different aspects of the same conflict, an expression is needed to cover the whole; "revolutionary war" will serve the purpose.

Chapter 1

REVOLUTIONARY WAR: NATURE AND CHARACTERISTICS

WHAT IS A REVOLUTIONARY WAR?

A revolutionary war is primarily an internal conflict, although external influences seldom fail to bear upon it. Although in many cases, the insurgents have been easily identifiable national groups—Indonesians, Vietnamese, Tunisians, Algerians, Congolese, Angolans today—this does not alter the strategically important fact that they were challenging a *local* ruling power controlling the existing administration, police, and armed forces. In this respect, colonial revolutionary wars have not differed from the purely indigenous ones, such as those in Cuba and South Vietnam.

The conflict results from the action of the insurgent aiming to seize power—or at splitting off from the existing country, as the Kurds are attempting to do now—and from the reaction of the counterinsurgent aiming to keep his power. At this point, significant differences begin to emerge between the two camps. Whereas in conventional war, either side can initiate the conflict, only one—the insurgent—can initiate a revolutionary war, for counterinsurgency is only an effect of insurgency. Furthermore, counterinsurgency cannot be defined except by reference to its cause.

Paraphrasing Clausewitz, we might say that "Insurgency is the pursuit of the policy of a party, inside a country, by every means." It is not like an ordinary war—a "continuation of the policy by other means"—because an insurgency can start long before the insurgent resorts to the use of force.

REVOLUTION, PLOT, INSURGENCY

Revolution, plot (or *coup d'état*), and insurgency are the three ways to take power by force. It will be useful to our analysis to try to distinguish among them.

A revolution usually is an explosive upheaval—sudden, brief, spontaneous, unplanned (France, 1789; China, 1911; Russia, 1917; Hungary, 1956). It is an *accident,* which can be explained afterward but not predicted other than to note the existence of a revolutionary situation. How and exactly when the explosion will occur cannot be forecast. A revolutionary situation exists today in Iran. Who can tell what will happen, whether there will be an explosion, and if so, how and when it will erupt?

In a revolution, masses move and then leaders appear. Sun Yat-sen was in England when the Manchu dynasty was overthrown, Lenin in Switzerland when the Romanovs fell.

A plot is the clandestine action of an insurgent group directed at the overthrow of the top leadership in its country. Because of its clandestine nature, a plot cannot and does not involve the masses. Although preparations for the plot may be long, the action itself is brief and sudden. A plot is always a *gamble* (the plot against Hitler in 1944; the plots in Iraq against King Faisal and Nuri al-Said in 1958, and against Kassem in 1963).

On the other hand, an insurgency is a *protracted struggle* conducted methodically, step by step, in order to attain specific intermediate objectives leading finally to the overthrow of the existing order (China, 1927–49; Greece, 1945–50; Indochina, 1945–54; Malaya, 1948–60; Algeria, 1954–62). To be sure, it can no more be predicted than a revolution; in fact, its beginnings are so vague that to determine exactly when an insurgency starts is a difficult legal, political, and historical problem. In China, for instance, should it be dated from 1927, when the Kuomintang-Communist alliance broke and force came into play, or from 1921, when the Chinese Communist Party was founded to establish a Communist regime in the country? But though it cannot be predicted, an insurgency is usually slow to develop and is not an accident, for in an insurgency leaders appear and then the masses are made to move. Although all recent insurgencies—with the exception of that in Greece—were clearly tied to a revolutionary situation, the cases of Malaya (1948–60), Tunisia (1952–55), Morocco (1952–56), Cyprus (1955–59), Cuba (1957–59), and others seem to show that the revolutionary situation did not have to be acute in order for the insurgency to be initiated.

INSURGENCY AND CIVIL WAR

An insurgency is a civil war. Yet there is a difference in the form the war takes in each case.

A civil war suddenly splits a nation into two or more groups which, after a brief period of initial confusion, find themselves in control of part of both the territory and the existing armed forces that they proceed immediately to develop. The war between these groups soon resembles an ordinary international war except that the opponents are fellow citizens, such as in the American War Between the States and the Spanish Civil War.

ASYMMETRY BETWEEN THE INSURGENT AND
THE COUNTERINSURGENT

There is an asymmetry between the opposite camps of a revolutionary war. This phenomenon results from the very nature of the war, from the disproportion of strength between the opponents at the outset, and from the difference in essence between their assets and their liabilities.

Since the insurgent alone can initiate the conflict (which is not to say that he is necessarily the first to use force), strategic initiative is his by definition. He is free to choose his hour, to wait safely for a favorable situation, unless external factors force him to accelerate his moves. However, in the world of today, polarized as it is between East and West, no revolutionary war can remain a purely internal affair. It is probable that the Malayan and the Indonesian Communist Parties were ordered to start the violent phase of their insurgency at the 1948 Calcutta Communist-sponsored Conference of Youth and Students of Southeast Asia. Thus, the decision was not entirely left to the Malayan and Indonesian Parties.

Until the insurgent has clearly revealed his intentions by engaging in subversion or open violence, he represents nothing but an imprecise, potential menace to the counterinsurgent and does not offer a concrete target that would justify a large effort. Yet an insurgency can reach a high degree of development by legal and peaceful means, at least in countries where political opposition is tolerated. This greatly limits pre-emptive moves on the part of the counterinsurgent. Usually, the most he can do is to try to eliminate or alleviate the conditions propitious for an insurgency.

An appraisal of the contending forces at the start of a revolutionary war shows an overwhelming superiority in tangible assets in favor of the counterinsurgent. Endowed with the normal foreign and domestic perquisites of an established government, he has virtually everything—diplomatic recognition; legitimate power in the executive, legislative, and judicial branches; control of the administration and police; financial resources; industrial and agricultural resources at home or ready access to them abroad; transport and communications facilities; use and control of the information and propaganda media; command of the armed forces and the possibility of increasing their size. He is *in* while the insurgent, being *out,* has none or few of these assets.

The situation is reversed in the field of intangibles. The insurgent has a formidable asset—the ideological power of a cause on which to base his action. The counterinsurgent has a heavy liability—he is responsible for maintaining order throughout the country. The insurgent's strategy will naturally aim at converting his intangible assets into concrete ones, the counterinsurgent's strategy at preventing his intangible liability from dissipating his concrete assets.

The insurgent thus has to grow in the course of the war from small to large, from weakness to strength, or else he fails. The counterinsurgent will decline from large to small, from strength to weakness, in direct relation to the insurgent's success.

The peculiarities that mark the revolutionary war as so different from the conventional one derive from this initial asymmetry.

OBJECTIVE: THE POPULATION

Afflicted with his congenital weakness, the insurgent would be foolish if he mustered whatever forces were available to him and attacked his opponent in a conventional fashion, taking as his objective the destruction of the enemy's forces and the conquest of the territory. Logic forces him instead to carry the fight to a different ground where he has a better chance to balance the physical odds against him.

The population represents this new ground. If the insurgent manages to dissociate the population from the counterinsurgent, to control it physically, to get its active support, he will win the war because, in the final analysis, the exercise of political power depends on the tacit or explicit agreement of the population or, at worst, on its submissiveness.

Thus the battle for the population is a major characteristic of the revolutionary war.

REVOLUTIONARY WAR IS A POLITICAL WAR

All wars are theoretically fought for a political purpose, although in some cases the final political outcome differs greatly from the one intended initially.

In the conventional war, military action, seconded by diplomacy, propaganda, and economic pressure, is generally the principal way to achieve the goal. Politics *as an instrument of war* tends to take a back seat and emerges again—as an instrument—when the fighting ends. We are not implying that politics vanishes entirely as the main directing force but rather that, in the course of the conventional war, once political goals have been set (although the government may change them), once directives have been given to the armed forces (although the government may modify them), military action becomes foremost. *"La parole passe aux armes";* the gun becomes the *"ultima ratio regum."* With the advent of the nuclear age and its consequent risks of mutual destruction, politics, no doubt, will interfere more closely—as it did in the recent case of Korea—with the conduct of the war (limited objectives) and with the actual conduct of the operations (privileged sanctuaries, exclusion of nuclear weapons). Nevertheless, military action remains the principal instrument of the conventional war.

As a result, it is relatively easy to allocate tasks and responsibilities among the government, which directs operations, the population, which provides the tools, and the soldier, who utilizes them.

The picture is different in the revolutionary war. The objective being the population itself, the operations designed to win it over (for the insurgent) or to keep it at least submissive (for the counterinsurgent) are essentially of a political nature. In this case, consequently, political action remains foremost throughout the war. It is not enough for the government to set political goals, to determine how much military force is applicable, to enter into alliances or to break them; *politics becomes an active instrument of operation.* And so intricate is the interplay between the political and the military actions that they cannot be tidily separated; on the contrary, every military move has to be weighed with regard to its political effects, and vice versa.

The insurgent, whose political establishment is a party and whose armed forces are the party's forces, enjoys an obvious advantage over his opponent, whose political establishment is the country's government, which may or may not be supported by a party or by a coalition of parties with their centrifugal tendencies, and whose army is the nation's army, reflecting the consensus or the lack of consensus in the nation.

GRADUAL TRANSITION FROM PEACE TO WAR

In the conventional war, the aggressor who has prepared for it within the confines of his national territory, channeling his resources into the preparation, has much to gain by attacking suddenly with all his forces. The transition from peace to war is as abrupt as the state of the art allows; the first shock may be decisive.

This is hardly possible in the revolutionary war because the aggressor— the insurgent—lacks sufficient strength at the outset. Indeed, years may sometimes pass before he has built up significant political, let alone military, power. So there is usually little or no first shock, little or no surprise, no possibility of an early decisive battle.

In fact, the insurgent has no interest in producing a shock until he feels fully able to withstand the enemy's expected reaction. By delaying the moment when the insurgency appears as a serious challenge to the counterinsurgent, the insurgent delays the reaction. The delay may be further prolonged by exploiting the fact that the population realizes the danger even later than the counterinsurgent leadership.

REVOLUTIONARY WAR IS A PROTRACTED WAR

The protracted nature of a revolutionary war does not result from a design by either side; it is imposed on the insurgent by his initial weakness. It takes time for a small group of insurgent leaders to organize a revolutionary movement, to raise and to develop armed forces, to reach a balance with the opponent, and to overpower him. A revolutionary war is short only if the counterinsurgency collapses at an early stage, as in Cuba, where the Batista regime disintegrated suddenly, less under the blows from the insurgents than through its own weakness; or if, somehow, a political settlement is reached, as in Tunisia, Morocco, Cyprus. To date, there has never been an early collapse of an insurgency.

The revolutionary war in China lasted twenty-two years, if 1927 is taken as the starting year. The war lasted five years in Greece, nine in Indochina, nine in the Philippines, five in Indonesia, twelve in Malaya, three in Tunisia, four in Morocco, eight in Algeria. The war started in 1948 in Burma and still goes on, though in a feeble way.

INSURGENCY IS CHEAP, COUNTERINSURGENCY COSTLY

Promoting disorder is a legitimate objective for the insurgent. It helps to disrupt the economy, hence to produce discontent; it serves to undermine the strength and the authority of the counterinsurgent. Moreover, disorder—the normal state of nature—is cheap to create and very costly to prevent. The insurgent blows up a bridge, so every bridge has to be guarded; he throws a grenade in a movie theater, so every person entering a public place has to be searched. When the insurgent burns a farm, all the farmers clamor for protection; if they do not receive it, they may be tempted to deal privately with the insurgent, as happened in Indochina and Algeria, to give just two examples. Merely by making anonymous phone calls warning of bombs planted in luggage, the insurgent can disrupt civilian airline schedules and scare away tourists.

Because the counterinsurgent cannot escape the responsibility for maintaining order, the ratio of expenses between him and the insurgent is high. It may be ten or twenty to one, or higher. The figure varies greatly, of course, from case to case, and in each situation during the course of the revolutionary war. It seems to apply particularly when the insurgent reaches the initial stages of violence and resorts to terrorism and guerrilla warfare. The British calculated the cost of every rebel in Malaya at more than $200,000. In Algeria, the FLN budget at its peak amounted to $30 or $40 million a year, less than the French forces had to spend in two weeks.

There is, it seems, an upper limit to this ratio. When the insurgent increases his terrorism or guerrilla activity by a factor of two, three, or five, he does not force the counterinsurgent to multiply his expenditures by the same factor. Sooner or later, a saturation point is reached, a point where the law of diminishing returns operates for both sides.

Once the insurgent has succeeded in acquiring stable geographical bases, as, for instance, the Chinese Communists did in northwest China, or the Vietminh in Tonkin, he becomes *ipso facto* a strong promoter of order within his own area, in order to show the difference between the effectiveness of his rule and the inadequacy of his opponent's.

Because of the disparity in cost and effort, the insurgent can thus accept a protracted war; the counterinsurgent should not.

FLUIDITY OF THE INSURGENT, RIGIDITY OF THE COUNTERINSURGENT

The insurgent is fluid because he has neither responsibility nor concrete assets; the counterinsurgent is rigid because he has both, and no amount of wailing can alter this fact for either side. Each must accept the situation as it is and make the best of it.

If the counterinsurgent wanted to rid himself of his rigidity, he would have to renounce to some extent his claim to the effective rule of the country, or dispose of his concrete assets. One way of doing this, of course, would be to hand over everything to the insurgent, and then start an insurgency against him, but no counterinsurgent on record has dared apply this extreme solution.

On the other hand, the insurgent is obliged to remain fluid at least until he has reached a balance of forces with the counterinsurgent. However desirable for the insurgent to possess territory, large regular forces, and powerful weapons, to possess them and to rely on them prematurely could spell his doom. The failure of the Greek Communist insurgents may be attributed in part to the risk they took when they organized their forces into battalions, regiments, and divisions, and accepted battle. The Vietminh made the same mistake in 1951 in Tonkin, and suffered serious set backs.

In the revolutionary war, therefore, and until the balance of forces has been reached, only the insurgent can consistently wage profitable hit-and-run operations because the counterinsurgent alone offers profitable and fixed targets; only the insurgent, as a rule, is free to accept or refuse battle, the counterinsurgent being bound by his responsibility. On the other hand, only the counterinsurgent can use substantial means because he alone possesses them.

Fluidity for one side and rigidity for the other are further determined by the nature of the operations. They are relatively simple for the insurgent—promoting disorder in every way until he assumes power; they are complicated for the counterinsurgent, who has to take into account conflicting demands (protection of the population and the economy, and offensive operations against the insurgent) and who has to coordinate all the components of his forces—the administrator, the policeman, the soldier, the social worker, etc. The insurgent can afford a loose, primitive organization; he can delegate a wide margin of initiative, but his opponent cannot.

THE POWER OF IDEOLOGY

The insurgent cannot seriously embark on an insurgency unless he has a well-grounded cause with which to attract supporters among the population. A cause, as we have seen, is his sole asset at the beginning, and it must be a powerful one if the insurgent is to overcome his weakness.

Can two explosive but antagonistic causes exist simultaneously in a single country—one for the insurgent, the other for his opponent? Such a situation has happened occasionally, for example, in the United States, when the antislavery movement clashed with the doctrine of states' rights. The most likely result in this case is a civil war, not an insurgency.

The probability is that only one cause exists. If the insurgent has preempted it, then the force of ideology works for him and not for the counterinsurgent. However, this is true largely in the early parts of the conflict. Later on, as the war develops, war itself becomes the paramount issue, and the original cause consequently loses some of its importance.

It has been asserted that a counterinsurgent confronted by a dynamic insurgent ideology is bound to meet defeat, that no amount of tactics and technique can compensate for his ideological handicap. This is not necessarily so because the population's attitude in the middle stage of the war is dictated not so much by the relative popularity and merits of the opponents as by the more primitive concern for safety. Which side gives the best protection, which one threatens the most, which one is likely to win, these are the criteria governing the population's stand. So much the better, of course, if popularity and effectiveness are combined.

PROPAGANDA—A ONE-SIDED WEAPON

The asymmetrical situation has important effects on propaganda. The insurgent, having no responsibility, is free to use every trick; if necessary, he can lie, cheat, exaggerate. He is not obliged to prove; he is judged by what he promises, not by what he does. Consequently, propaganda is a powerful weapon for him. With no positive policy but with good propaganda, the insurgent may still win.

The counterinsurgent is tied to his responsibilities and to his past, and for him, facts speak louder than words. He is judged on what he does, not on what he says. If he lies, cheats, exaggerates, and does not prove, he may achieve some temporary successes, but at the price of being discredited for good. And he cannot cheat much unless his political structures are monolithic, for the legitimate opposition in his own camp would soon disclose his every psychological maneuver. For him, propaganda can be no more than a secondary weapon, valuable only if intended to inform and not to fool. A counterinsurgent can seldom cover bad or nonexistent policy with propaganda.

REVOLUTIONARY WAR REMAINS
UNCONVENTIONAL UNTIL THE END

Once the insurgent has acquired strength and possesses significant regular forces, it would seem that the war should become a conventional one, a sort of civil war in which each camp holds a portion of the national territory from which he directs blows at the other. But if the insurgent has understood his strategic problems well, revolutionary war never reverts to a conventional form.

For one reason, the creation of a regular army by the insurgent does not mean an end to subversion and guerrilla activity. On the contrary, they increase in scope and intensity in order to facilitate the operations of the regular army and to amplify their effects.

For another reason, the insurgent has involved the population in the conflict since its beginning; the active participation of the population was indeed a *sine qua non* for his success. Having acquired the decisive advantage of a population organized and mobilized on his side, why should he cease to make use of an asset that gives his regular forces the fluidity and the freedom of action that the counterinsurgent cannot achieve? As long as the population remains under his control, the insurgent retains his liberty to refuse battle except on his own terms.

In 1947, the Chinese Nationalists launched an offensive against Yenan, the Communist capital, in northern Shensi. They took it without difficulty; the Communist Government and regular forces evacuated the area without a fight. Soon after, however, the population, the local militias, and a small core of guerrilla and regional troops began harassing the Nationalists while regular Communist units attacked their long communication lines, which extended north from Sian. The Nationalists were finally obliged to withdraw, having gained nothing and lost much in the affair.

In 1953, the French forces in Indochina found a study made by the Vietminh command to determine whether in Vietminh territory there was any area, any fixed installation worth defending. The answer was no. Indeed, that same year, in Vietminh territory northwest of Hanoi, the French seized a huge depot of trucks and ammunitions left totally unguarded.

We have indicated above the general characteristics of revolutionary war. They are an ineluctable product of the nature of this war. An insurgent or a counterinsurgent who would conduct his war in opposition to any of these characteristics, going against the grain, so to speak, would certainly not increase his chances for success.

Chapter 2

THE PREREQUISITES FOR
A SUCCESSFUL INSURGENCY

The cause of most recent insurgencies can easily be attributed to revolutionary situations that might have exploded into spontaneous revolutions but bred instead a group of leaders who then proceeded to organize and conduct the insurgencies. In view of this fact, it would be wrong and unjust to conclude that insurgencies are merely the product of personal ambitions on the part of their leaders who developed the whole movement, artificially, so to speak.

For the sake of demonstration, let us suppose that in Country X a small group of discontented men—possessing the attributes of leadership, inspired by the success of so many insurgencies in the past twenty years, well aware of the strategic and tactical problems involved in such an enterprise—have met and decided to overthrow the existing order by the path of insurgency.

In light of the counterinsurgent's material superiority at the outset, their chances of victory will obviously depend on whether certain preliminary conditions are met. What conditions? Are these conditions a must? In other words, what are the prerequisites for a successful insurgency?

Knowing what they are would help in assessing, from a counterinsurgent's point of view, how vulnerable a country would be to an insurgency.

A CAUSE

Necessity of a Cause

How can the insurgent ever hope to pry the population away from the counterinsurgent, to control it, and to mobilize it? By finding supporters among the population, people whose support will range from active participation in the struggle to passive approval. The first basic need for an insurgent who aims at more than simply making trouble is an attractive cause, particularly in view of the risks involved and in view of the fact that the early supporters and the active supporters—not necessarily the same persons—have to be recruited by persuasion.

With a cause, the insurgent has a formidable, if intangible, asset that he can progressively transform into concrete strength. A small group of men *sans* cause can seize power by a lucky plot—this has happened in history—but then a plot is not an insurgency. The lack of an attractive cause is what restrains a priori apolitical crime syndicates from attempting to assume power, for they realize that only criminals will follow them.

The 1945–50 Communist insurgency in Greece, a textbook case of everything that can go wrong in an insurgency, is an example of failure due, among other less essential reasons, to the lack of a cause. The Communist Party, the EAM, and its army, the ELAS, grew during World War II, when the entire population was resisting the Germans. Once the country was liberated, the EAM could find no valid cause. Greece had little industry and consequently no proletariat except the dockers of Piraeus and tobacco-factory workers; the merchant sailors, whose jobs kept them moving about, could provide no constant support. There was no appalling agrarian problem to exploit. The wealthy Greek capitalists, whose fortunes had usually been made abroad, were an object of admiration rather than of hostility in a trade-minded nation. No sharply fixed classes existed; the Minister of the Navy might well be the cousin of a café waiter. To make matters worse, the Greek Communists were perforce allied to Bulgaria, Greece's traditional enemy; to Yugoslavia, which claims a part of Greece's Macedonia; to Albania, from which Greece claims part of Epirus. With national feelings running as high as they do in the Balkans, these associations did not increase the popularity of the Greek Communists.

Using what forces they had at the end of the war, taking advantage of the difficult terrain, withdrawing into safe asylum across the satellites' borders when necessary, the Communist insurgents were able to wage commando-type operations but not true guerrilla warfare; in fact, their infiltrating units had to hide from the population when they could not cow it, and their operations lasted generally as long as the supplies they carried with them. The ELAS was obliged to enlist partisans by force. Whenever the unwilling recruits found the political commissar behind their back less dangerous than the nationalist forces in front, they deserted.

The main reason the insurgency lasted so long was that, at the start, the regular government forces consisted of only a single brigade, which had fought with the Allies in the Mediterranean Theater and was greatly outnumbered by the insurgents. As soon as the army was reorganized and strengthened, first with British, then with U.S. aid, the nationalist command undertook to clean the country area by area, by purely military action. A cleaned area was kept clean by arming local militias; this presented little difficulty since the population was definitely anti-Communist and could be relied upon.

Strategic Criteria of a Cause

The best cause for the insurgent's purpose is one that, by definition, can attract the largest number of supporters and repel the minimum of opponents. Thus, a cause appealing to the proletariat in an industrialized country (or to the peasants in an underdeveloped one) is a good cause. A purely Negro movement trying to exploit the Negro problem as a basis for an insurgency in the United States (with a population of 20 million Negroes and 160 million whites) would be doomed from the start. In South Africa (with 11 million Negroes and 4 million whites), its chances would be good—other factors aside. Independence from colonial rule was automatically a good cause in Indonesia, Indochina, Tunisia, Morocco, Algeria, Cyprus, the Belgian Congo, and now Angola.

The insurgent must, of course, be able to identify himself totally with the cause or, more precisely, with the entire majority of the population theoretically attracted by it. In Malaya, independence from Great Britain was the cause chosen by the insurgents, the Malayan Communist Party. However, 90 percent of the Party members were Chinese, not true Malays; the Malays consequently remained largely indifferent to the struggle. The same story occurred in Kenya (if one chooses to qualify what took place there as a revolutionary war; the insurgency was conducted in so crude a fashion as to make its inclusion in this category questionable). Independence was pursued by members of a single tribe, the Kikuyus; no other tribe moved in support.

To be perfectly sound, the cause must be such that the counterinsurgent cannot espouse it too or can do so only at the risk of losing his power, which is, after all, what he is fighting for. Land reform looked like a promising cause to the Hukbalahaps after the defeat of Japan and the accession of the Philippines to independence; but when the government offered land to the Huks' actual and potential supporters, the insurgents lost their cause and the game. The same disaster struck the Malayan Communist Party, once Britain promised independence to the country and set a date for it.

A cause, finally, must also be lasting, if not for the duration of the revolutionary war, at least until the insurgent movement is well on its feet. This differentiates a strategic cause from a tactical one, a deep-seated cause from a temporary one resulting from the exploitation of an ephemeral difficulty, such as, for instance, the high price and the scarcity of food after a year of natural calamities.

The Nature of the Cause

What is a political problem? It is "an unsolved contradiction," according to Mao Tse-tung. If one accepts this definition, then a political cause is the championing of one side of the contradiction. In other words, where there is no problem, there is no cause, but there are always problems in any country. What makes one country more vulnerable than another to insurgency is the depth and the acuity of its existing problems.

Problems of all natures are exploitable for an insurgency, provided the causes they lead to meet the above criteria. The problem may be essentially political, related to the national or international situation of the country. The dictatorship of Batista for the Cuban insurgents, the Japanese aggression for the Chinese are examples of political problems. It follows that any country where the power is invested in an oligarchy, whether indigenous or foreign, is potential ground for a revolutionary war.

The problem may be social, as when one class is exploited by another or denied any possibility of improving its lot. This has been exhaustively discussed since Karl Marx, and little need be added here. The problem becomes particularly dangerous when the society does not integrate those who, by the level of their education or by their achievements, have proved to belong to the true elite. For it is among this rejected elite that the insurgents can find the indispensable leaders.

The problem may be economic, such as the low price of agricultural products in relation to industrial goods, or the low price of raw material in relation to finished products, or the import of foreign goods rather than the development of a national industry. The issue of neocolonialism today is closely related to this problem.

The problem may be racial, as it would be in South Africa. Or religious, as it would be in Lebanon, although here the population is evenly divided between Christians and Moslems. Or cultural, as in India, where the multiplicity of languages has already produced considerable agitation.

The problem may even be artificial so long as it has a chance to be accepted as a fact. The lot of the Chinese farmers—victims of exactions by the authorities and of the rapacity of the local usurers—was no doubt a hard one. The Chinese Communists did exploit this problem. However, their chief cause, borrowed from Sun Yat-sen, was land reform. Its revolutionary value lies in the idea that land ownership was concentrated in a small minority; a class war on the issue would theoretically bring to their side the majority of the farmers. The sole comprehensive work on the subject of land tenure in China, by J. Lossing Buck, contradicted the Communist picture of the situation,[1] but this fact did not decrease in the slightest the psychological value of the slogan "Land to the Tiller." An efficient propaganda machine can turn an artificial problem into a real one.

It is not absolutely necessary that the problem be acute, although the insurgent's work is facilitated if such is the case. If the problem is merely latent, the first task of the insurgent is to make it acute by "raising the political consciousness of the masses." Terrorism may be a quick means of producing this effect. Batista's dictatorship did not by itself suddenly become unbearable to the Cuban people; they had lived under other dictatorships in the past, including a previous Batista regime. And the country was prosperous in 1958, although there was great disparity in the distribution of wealth. Batista might perhaps have lasted many more years had it not been for Castro and his followers, who spectacularly raised the issue and focused the latent opposition on their movement.

Tactical Manipulation of the Cause

The insurgent is not restricted to the choice of a single cause. Unless he has found an over-all cause, like anticolonialism, which is sufficient in itself because it combines all the political, social, economic, racial, religious, and cultural causes described above, he has much to gain by selecting an assortment of causes especially tailored for the various groups in the society that he is seeking to attract.

Let us suppose that the revolutionary movement is tentatively made up, as it was in China, of the Communist Party ("vanguard of the revolution, party of the workers and the poor farmers") and its allies (medium and rich peasants, artisans, plus the "national bourgeoisie" and the capitalists who suffer from "bureaucratic capitalism" and from the economic encroachments of the imperialists). The insurgent has to appeal to the whole, and a cause is necessary for that. Since it is easier to unite "against" than "for," particularly when the components are so varied, the general cause will most probably be a negative one, something like "throw the rascals out" (the rascals in this case: Chiang Kai-shek and the Kuomintang reactionaries; the feudal warlords; "bureaucratic capitalism"; the compradores, "running dogs of imperialism"; and the landlords). In addition, the insurgent must appeal to each component of the movement, and in this aspect, the various causes will probably contain a constructive element: for the proletariat, a Marxist society; for the poor farmers, land; for the medium farmers, fair taxes; for the rich farmers, just, reasonable, and lasting settlement; for the national bourgeoisie, defense of the national interests, order, fair taxes, development of trade and industry, protection against imperialist competition.

Nothing obliges the insurgent to stick to the same cause if another one looks more profitable. Thus, in China, the Communists initially took the classic Marxist stand in favor of the workers (1921–25). Then they actively espoused the national cause of the Kuomintang, for the unification of China against the warlords (1925–27). After the Kuomintang–Communist split, they largely dropped the workers in favor of the poor peasants, advocating land reform by radical means (1928–34). Then Japanese aggression became the central issue in China, and the Communists advocated a patriotic united front against Japan (1927–45), adopting meanwhile a moderate agrarian policy: Land redistribution would be ended, but instead, the Communists would impose strict control of rents and interest rates. After the Japanese surrender, they finally reverted to land reform with the temperate proviso that landlords themselves would be entitled to a share of land (1945–49). What the Communists actually did after their victory, between 1950 and 1952, was to carry out their land reform "through violent struggles" in order to conduct a class war among the rural population and thereby definitely to commit the activists on their side, if only because these activists had shared in the crimes. Once this was achieved, the Party buried land reform for good and started collectivizing the land.

Thus, if idealism and a sense of ethics weigh in favor of a consistent stand, tactics pull toward opportunism.

Diminishing Importance of the Cause

The importance of a cause, an absolute essential at the outset of an insurgency, decreases progressively as the insurgent acquires strength. The war itself becomes the principal issue, forcing the population to take sides, preferably the winning one. This has already been explained in the previous chapter.

WEAKNESS OF THE COUNTERINSURGENT

Let us assume now that our minute group of insurgent leaders in Country X has found several good causes, some acute, some latent, some even artificial, on which to base their insurgency. They all have agreed on a potent platform. Can they start operating? Not unless another preliminary condition has been met. The insurgent, starting from almost zero while his enemy still has every means at his disposal, is as vulnerable as a new-born baby. He cannot live and grow without some sort of protection, and who but the counterinsurgent himself can protect him? Therefore, we must analyze what makes a body politic resistant to infection.

Strengths and Weaknesses of the Political Regime

1. *Absence of problems.* A country fortunate enough to know no problem is obviously immune from insurgency. But since we have assumed that our potential insurgent leaders have found a cause, let us eliminate these countries—if there are any—from our consideration.

2. *National consensus.* The solidity of a regime is primarily based upon this factor. Thailand may live under a dictatorship or a democratic system, but her national consensus—which is not apathy, for the Thais would react vigorously to any attempt against their King and their way of life—has so far always strengthened the regime in power. On the other hand, no national consensus backs up East Germany's government.

3. *Resoluteness of the counterinsurgent leadership.* Resoluteness is a major factor in any sort of conflict, but particularly so in a revolutionary war for the reasons that (a) the insurgent has the initial benefit of a dynamic cause; (b) an insurgency does not grow suddenly into a national danger and the people's reaction against it is slow. Consequently, the role of the counterinsurgent leaders is paramount.

4. *Counterinsurgent leaders' knowledge of counterinsurgency warfare.* It is not enough for the counterinsurgent leaders to be resolute; they must also be aware of the strategy and tactics required in fighting an insurgency. Generalissimo Chiang Kai-shek's determination cannot be questioned; he proved it against Japan and still shows it in Taiwan. But did he know how to cope with the Communists' methods?

5. *The machine for the control of the population.* Four instruments of control count in a revolutionary war situation: the political structure, the administrative bureaucracy, the police, the armed forces.

    a. *The political structure.* If Country X is located behind the Iron Curtain, where political opposition is not tolerated and where the population is kept under a system of terror and mutual suspicion, the initial group of insurgents has no chance to develop; at best, the group will be able to survive in total secrecy—and hence be completely inactive—while waiting for better times.

Since there are people who dream of unleashing insurgencies in certain Communist countries—"Don't the people hate the regime there?"—it may be useful to give an idea of the extent of population control achieved by the Communist techniques of terror and mutual suspicion, of which the Red Chinese are past masters.

In Canton, in 1954, a neighbor saw an old Chinese lady giving some rice to her cat.

"I am sorry, but I will be obliged to report you at the next street meeting," said the neighbor to the owner of the cat.

"Why?" asked the old lady.

"Because rice is rationed and you have been wasting it on your cat."

"If you report me, they will cut off my rice ration. Why don't you just keep silent?"

"Suppose someone else saw you and reports you. What will happen to me, your neighbor, if I have not reported you first? I am your friend. If they suppress your ration I will give you half of mine."

This is exactly what happened, in a city where, according to some Western visitors, Chinese Communist control was less efficient than elsewhere in China.

At the end of 1952, a European was expelled from Hainan Island, where he had lived for many years. On reaching Hong Kong, he reported that the peasants "hated" the regime, and he gave much convincing evidence of it. He mentioned later that the Nationalists had twice attempted to drop agents in his area from Taiwan. In each case, the militia on duty at night heard the planes, saw the parachutes coming down, gave the alert, and the Nationalist agents were cornered and captured by several hundred armed villagers.

The European was challenged on this: "Isn't there a contradiction between your statement concerning the feelings of the peasants toward the regime and the attitude of the militiamen, who, after all, are peasants too? Why didn't they keep silent?"

"Put yourself in the place of one of these militiamen," he explained. "How does he know whether the other members of the militia won't give the alert? If they do and he hasn't, he will be in great trouble when the Communist cadres make their usual post-mortem investigations."

In July, 1953, during the Korean War, the Nationalists decided to make a raid on the mainland of China. They selected as their objective the small peninsula of Tungshan, jutting out of the Fukien coast, which is transformed into an island at high tide. The Communist garrison was made up of a regular battalion plus a thousand-man militia. The latter, the Nationalists thought, would put up no real fight. Indeed, every piece of available intelligence indicated that the population was thoroughly fed up with the Communists. The plan was to drop a regiment of paratroopers to neutralize the Communist battalion and to control the isthmus in order to prevent reinforcement from the mainland; an amphibious landing would follow to wipe out the opposition.

Because of a miscalculation in computing the local tide, the amphibious landing was delayed, and the Nationalist paratroopers bore the brunt of the opposition alone. They were virtually annihilated. The militia fought like devils. How could they act otherwise when they knew that the Nationalist action was just a raid?

A control of this order rules out the possibility of launching an insurgency. As long as there is no privacy, as long as every unusual move or event is reported and checked, as long as parents are afraid to talk in front of their children, how can contacts be made, ideas spread, recruiting accomplished?

What is possible is terrorism in a limited way, because a single man, even though completely isolated, can conduct a terrorist campaign; witness the case of the "mad bomber" in New York. But terrorism itself has far less value than the publicity that it is expected to produce, and it is rather doubtful that Communist authorities would complacently furnish publicity.

Another tactic that continues to be possible was one used in Greece by the Communists—unsustained commandotype operations where terrain conditions are favorable.

At the other extreme, if anarchy prevails in Country X, the insurgent will find all the facilities he needs in order to meet, to travel, to contact people, to make known his program, to find and organize the early supporters, to receive and to distribute funds, to agitate and to subvert, or to launch a widespread campaign of terrorism.

In between these extremes lies a wide range of political structures that in varying degrees facilitate or hinder the task of the insurgent: dictatorship with a one-party system, dictatorship with no link to the grass roots, vigilant democracy, indolent democracy, etc.

  b. *The administrative bureaucracy.* A country is run in its day-to-day life by its bureaucracy, which has a force of its own that has sometimes no relation to the strength or weakness of the top political leadership. France under the Third and Fourth Republics had a weak leadership but a strong administrative apparatus; the opposite appears to be the case in South Vietnam today. Since an insurgency is a bottom-to-top movement, an administrative vacuum at the bottom, an incompetent bureaucracy, plays into the hands of the insurgent.

The case of Algeria may be taken as an example. The territory was notoriously underadministered on the eve of the insurgency, not because the civil servants were incompetent but rather because the bureaucratic establishment had no relation to the size of the country and its population. Algeria (not counting the Sahara) extends more than 650 miles along the Mediterranean Sea and 350 miles inland, with an area of 115,000 square miles and a population of 10,500,000, of whom 1,200,000 are of European stock.

Under a governor general in Algiers, the territory was divided into three *départements* with seats in Oran, Algiers, and Constantine, each under a *préfet* assisted by a large staff. A *département* was in turn divided into *sous-préfectures;* for instance, in the *département* of Algiers, there was the *sous-préfecture* of Kabylia, with its seat in Tizi-Ouzou. Kabylia consisted of 5,000 square miles of rugged mountain terrain, with 1,200,000 inhabitants, of whom 90 per cent were Moslems.

The lower echelon in predominantly Moslem areas was the *commune-mixte* under a French administrator with 1 or 2 assistants and 5 gendarmes; the *commune-mixte* of Tigzirt, in Kabylia, measured 30 miles by 20 miles, with some 80,000 inhabitants.

At the lowest level was the *douar,* where the power of the state was embodied in a *garde-champêtre,* a native rural policeman armed with an old pistol in a holster on which shone a brass sign engraved with the awe-inspiring words: *"La Loi."* One such *douar* covered an area of 10 miles by 6 miles, with a population of 15,000 Kabylias.

With this setup, the insurgents had a field day.

> c. *The police.* The eye and the arm of the government in all matters pertaining to internal order, the police are obviously a key factor in the early stages of an insurgency; they are the first counterinsurgent organization that has to be infiltrated and neutralized.

Their efficiency depends on their numerical strength, the competency of their members, their loyalty toward the government, and, last but not least, on the backing they get from the other branches of the government—particularly the judicial system. If insurgents, though identified and arrested by the police, take advantage of the many normal safeguards built into the judicial system and are released, the police can do little. Prompt adaptation of the judicial system to the extraordinary conditions of an insurgency, an agonizing problem at best, is a necessity. Algeria may again serve as an example. The total police force in 1954 was less than 50,000, barely larger than the police force for the city of Paris. When the insurgency was brewing, the Algerian police gave timely warnings, which were not heeded. A year after the insurgency broke out, the French National Assembly finally granted the government the "special powers" required to deal with the situation. By that time, the police—particularly its Moslem members—had been engulfed in the chaos.

> d. *The armed forces.* Leaving aside the factors of strength applicable to the armed forces in all wars, those that are relevant in a revolutionary war are:

i. The numerical strength of the armed forces in relation to the size and the population of the country. An insurgency is a two-dimensional war fought for the control of the population. There is no front, no safe rear. No area, no significant segment of the population can be abandoned for long—unless the population can be trusted to defend itself. This is why a ratio of force of ten or twenty to one between the counterinsurgent and the insurgent is not uncommon when the insurgency develops into guerrilla warfare. The French forces in Indochina never approached this ratio, a fact that, more than any other, explains why the French could not have won there even if they had been led by Napoleon, regardless of the power of the nationalist cause initially.

ii. The composition of the armed forces. A conventional war today requires a modern, well-balanced force, with its air, sea, and ground components. But a revolutionary war is primarily a war of infantry. Paradoxically, the less sophisticated the counterinsurgent forces, the better they are. France's NATO divisions were useless in Algeria; their modern equipment had to be left behind, and highly specialized engineer or signal units had to be hurriedly converted into ordinary infantry. Naval operations by the insurgent being unlikely, all a navy needs is a sufficient force to blockade the coast line effectively. As for an air force, whose supremacy the insurgent cannot challenge, what it needs are slow assault fighters, short take-off transport planes, and helicopters.

iii. The feeling of the individual soldier toward the insurgent's cause and toward the counterinsurgent regime. Whereas the insurgent initially can use only a few combatants and can therefore select volunteers, the counterinsurgent's manpower demands are so high that he is condemned to draft soldiers, and he may well be plagued by the problem of loyalty. A few cases of collective desertions may cast so much suspicion on counterinsurgent units that their value may evaporate altogether. This happened with Algerian Rifle units in the early stage of the war in Algeria; although basically sound and trustworthy, these units had to be retired from direct contact with the population and used in a purely military capacity.

iv. The time lapse before intervention. Because of the gradual transition from peace to war in a revolutionary war, the armed forces are not ordered into action as fast as they would be in a conventional war. This delay is another characteristic of revolutionary wars. To reduce it is a political responsibility of the country's leaders.

6. *Geographic conditions.* Geography can weaken the strongest political regime or strengthen the weakest one. This question will subsequently be examined in more detail.

It is the combination of all these factors that determines whether an insurgency is possible or not once the potential insurgent has a cause.

Crisis and Insurgency

The insurgent cannot, of course, choose his opponent; he must accept him as he is. If he is confronted by a powerful counterinsurgent, he has no recourse but to wait until his opponent is weakened by some internal or external crisis.

The recent series of colonial insurgencies is, no doubt, a consequence of World War II, which constituted a formidable crisis for the colonial powers. The record shows that no insurgency or revolt succeeded in colonial territories before 1938, although the situation then was no less revolutionary than after the war. Few were even attempted—a revolt in the Dutch East Indies in 1926–27 and the extraordinary passive-resistance movement headed by Gandhi in India virtually exhaust the list.

The history of the Chinese Communist insurgency offers another example of the exploitation of a crisis. After a slow climb from 50 members in 1921 to 1,000 in 1925, the Chinese Communist Party associated itself with the Kuomintang, and its membership rose suddenly to 59,000 in 1926. The expansion was facilitated by the state of anarchy prevailing in China and by the popularity of the struggle led by the Kuomintang against the warlords and the imperialists. The two parties split in 1927, and the CCP went into open rebellion. Immediately, the membership fell to 10,000. A Communist group with Mao Tse-tung took refuge in the Kiangsi-Hunan area, while other groups scattered in various places. They slowly initiated guerrilla warfare, and, although at first they committed the mistake of attacking well-defended towns, they managed to develop their military strength. Membership rose to 300,000 in 1934. The Kuomintang had succeeded by that time in establishing itself as the central government of China, and the Communists alone presented a challenge to its authority. The Kuomintang, by now a strong power, was energetically trying to stamp out the rebellion. After several unsuccessful offensives against the Communists, the Nationalist forces pressed them so hard that the CCP was really fighting for its survival. In order to escape annihilation, the Communists set off on their Long March, from Kiangsi to a remote area in the north of Shensi. In 1937, after the Long March, membership had fallen again to 40,000. Chiang Kai-shek was preparing another powerful offensive to finish off the Reds when they were saved by a crisis, the Japanese aggression against China. By V-J day, the Party had grown to 1,200,000, controlled an area of 350,000 square miles with a population of 95 million, and had a regular army of 900,000 men and a militia force of 2,400,000. It was no longer vulnerable.

The Border Doctrine

Every country is divided for administrative and military purposes into provinces, counties, districts, zones, etc. The border areas are a permanent source of weakness for the counterinsurgent whatever his administrative structures, and this advantage is usually exploited by the insurgent, especially in the initial violent stages of the insurgency. By moving from one side of the border to the other, the insurgent is often able to escape pressure or, at least, to complicate operations for his opponent.

It was no accident that the Chinese Communist-dominated areas included the Shensi-Kansu-Ningsia Border Area, the Shansi-Chahar-Hopei Military Region, the Hopei-Shantung-Honan Military Region, and the Shansi-Hopei-Honan Military Region. Operating astride borders had become a matter of doctrine for them.

GEOGRAPHIC CONDITIONS

The role of geography, a large one in an ordinary war, may be overriding in a revolutionary war. If the insurgent, with his initial weakness, cannot get any help from geography, he may well be condemned to failure before he starts. Let us examine briefly the effects of the various geographic factors.

1. *Location.* A country isolated by natural barriers (sea, desert, forbidding mountain ranges) or situated among countries that oppose the insurgency is favorable to the counterinsurgent.

2. *Size.* The larger the country, the more difficult for a government to control it. Size can weaken even the most totalitarian regime; witness China's present troubles in Tibet.

3. *Configuration.* A country easy to compartmentalize hinders the insurgent. Thus the Greek national forces had an easy task cleaning the Peloponnesus peninsula. If the country is an archipelago, the insurgency cannot easily spread, as was the case in the Philippines. The Indonesian Government, which is not remarkable for its strength, managed nevertheless to stamp out rebellions in the Moluccas, Amboina, and other islands.

4. *International borders.* The length of the borders, particularly if the neighboring countries are sympathetic to the insurgents, as was the case in Greece, Indochina, and Algeria, favors the insurgent. A high proportion of coast line to inland borders helps the counterinsurgent because maritime traffic can be controlled with a limited amount of technical means, which the counterinsurgent possesses or is usually able to acquire. It was cheaper in money and manpower to suppress smuggling along the coast of Algeria than along the Tunisian and Moroccan borders, where the French Army had to build, maintain, and man an artificial fence.

5. *Terrain.* It helps the insurgent insofar as it is rugged and difficult, either because of mountains and swamps or because of the vegetation. The hills of Kiangsi, the mountains of Greece, the Sierra Maestra, the swamps of the Plain of Reeds in Cochinchina, the paddy fields of Tonkin, the jungle of Malaya gave a strong advantage to the insurgents. The Chinese Communists in Manchuria profitably used the time when the fields were covered with high kaoliang stalks.

On the other hand, the FLN was never able to operate for any sustained period in the vast expanses of the Sahara, with the French forces securing the oases and vital wells and air surveillance detecting every move and even traces of movement left on sand.

6. *Climate.* Contrary to the general belief, harsh climates favor the counterinsurgent forces, which have, as a rule, better logistical and operational facilities. This will be especially favorable if the counterinsurgent soldier is a native and, therefore, accustomed to the rigors of the climate. The rainy season in Indochina hampered the Vietminh more than it did the French. Winter in Algeria brought FLN activity to almost a standstill. Merely to keep scarce weapons and ammunition in good condition when one lives continuously in the open, as the guerrilla does, is a perpetual headache.

7. *Population.* The size of the population affects the revolutionary war in the same way as does the size of the country: the more inhabitants, the more difficult to control them. But this factor can be attenuated or enhanced by the density and the distribution of the population. The more scattered the population, the better for the insurgent; this is why counterinsurgents in Malaya, in Algeria, and in South Vietnam today have attempted to regroup the population (as in Cambodia in 1950–52). A high ratio of rural to urban population gives an advantage to the insurgent; the OAS in Algeria was doomed tactically because it could rely only on the European population, which was concentrated in cities, particularly Algiers and Oran. The control of a town, which is extremely dependent on outside supplies, requires smaller forces than the control of the same number of people spread over the countryside—except in the case of a mass uprising, which can never last long in any event.

8. *Economy.* The degree of development and sophistication of the economy can work both ways. A highly developed country is very vulnerable to a short and intense wave of terrorism. But if terrorism lasts, the disruption becomes such that the population may not be able to endure it and, consequently, may turn against the insurgent even when it was not initially hostile to him.

An underdeveloped country is less vulnerable to terrorism but much more open to guerrilla warfare, if only because the counterinsurgent cannot count on a good network of transport and communication facilities and because the population is more autarchic.

To sum up, the ideal situation for the insurgent would be a large land-locked country shaped like a blunt-tipped star, with jungle-covered mountains along the borders and scattered swamps in the plains, in a temperate zone with a large and dispersed rural population and a primitive economy. (See Figure 1.) The counterinsurgent would prefer a small island shaped like a pointed star, on which a cluster of evenly spaced towns are separated by desert, in a tropical or arctic climate, with an industrial economy. (See Figure 2.)

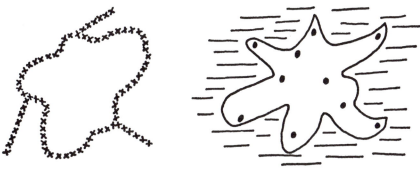

Figure 1.

Figure 2.

OUTSIDE SUPPORT

Outside support to an insurgency can take the form of:

1. *Moral support,* from which the insurgent will benefit without any effort on his part, provided his cause goes along with "the wind of history." Thus, in the present struggle between Angolans and the Portuguese Government, the former benefit from considerable moral support, while the latter is isolated. Moral support is expressed by the weight of public opinion and through various communications media. Propaganda is the chief instrument of moral support, used to sway public opinion when it is adverse, or to reinforce existing public sympathy.

2. *Political support,* with pressure applied directly on the counterinsurgent, or indirectly by diplomatic action in the international forum. Taking the same case as an example, we see that many African states have broken off diplomatic relations with Lisbon and recognized a provisional government of Angola; they have also succeeded in expelling Portugal from various international organizations such as the International Labor Organization.

3. *Technical support,* in the form of advice to the insurgent for the organization of his movement and the conduct of his political and military operations. The similarity between the Vietminh and the Chinese Communists' methods was not accidental.

4. *Financial support,* overt or covert. A great part of the FLN budget came from grants by the Arab League. Red China shipped tea to the FLN in Morocco, where it was sold on the open market.

5. *Military support,* either through direct intervention on the insurgent's side or by giving him training facilities and equipment.

No outside support is absolutely necessary at the start of an insurgency, although it obviously helps when available. Military support short of direct intervention, in particular, cannot be absorbed in a significant amount by the insurgent until his forces have reached a certain level of development. The initial military phase of an insurgency, whether terrorism or guerrilla warfare, requires little in the way of equipment, arms, ammunition, and explosives. These can usually be found locally or smuggled in.

When the time comes, however, for the insurgent to pass from guerrilla warfare to a higher form of operations, to create a regular army, the need for much larger and more varied supplies becomes acute. Either he is able to capture it from the counterinsurgent, or it must come from the outside. If not, the development of the insurgent military establishment is impossible.

The Communists in China received little or no support from abroad until Manchuria was occupied by the Soviet Army; the arms and equipment of the Japanese Kwantung Army were turned over to 100,000 soldiers from the People's Liberation Army who had crossed into Manchuria from Jehol and Shantung. The Communists in Manchuria were at once able to conduct large-scale sustained operations, and the nature of the fighting in this area was markedly different from the Communist operations south of the Great Wall. Access to the Japanese Army stores was not the decisive factor in the outcome of the war, since the Communist forces in China proper, who received few supplies from Manchuria, succeeded in arming themselves with captured Nationalist equipment; but it certainly hastened the defeat of the best Nationalist troops in Manchuria. The Communists boasted that their quartermaster and ordnance depots were conveniently located forward, in the hands of the Nationalists. Their slogan "Feed the War by War" was not an empty assertion.

In Indochina, the turning point occurred in 1950, when the Vietminh began receiving aid from Red China. Until then, they had been unable to develop their forces and to stage large-scale operations, not because they suffered from man power problems—they had more potential soldiers than they could use—but because their primitive arsenals could not fill their needs, and they could not capture significant amounts of French weapons. Although the Vietminh could have fought a protracted guerrilla warfare, and thus could have denied the French any benefit from a prolonged occupation of the country, they would not have been able to raise a powerful regular army without Chinese aid. By September, 1950, 20,000 men in the Vietminh forces had been equipped with machine guns, heavy mortars, anti-aircraft weapons. The Vietminh command was able to organize a Heavy Division, the 351st. In 1951, according to French estimates, Chinese aid amounted to 18,000 rifles, 1,200 machine guns, 150–200 heavy mortars, and about 50 recoilless guns.[2]

In Malaya and the Philippines, the insurgents received no outside military support and did not develop.

In Greece, the Communist insurgents received support from and through the satellite countries, but the split between Tito and Stalin interrupted the low just when the insurgents, having organized their forces into large—and vulnerable—units, needed it most.

In Algeria, the French naval blockade and the sealing of the borders prevented the flow of supplies to Algeria from Tunisia and Morocco, where large rebel stocks had been accumulated. No development was possible. The situation of the FLN forces after 1959 became so critical that most of their automatic weapons were buried for lack of ammunition.

The East-West conflict that today covers the entire world cannot fail to be affected by any insurgency occurring anywhere. Thus, a Communist insurgency is almost certain to receive automatic support from the Communist bloc. Chances for Communist support are good even for non-Communist insurgents, provided, of course, that their opponent is an "imperialist" or an ally of "imperialism."

Conversely, the East-West conflict sometimes accelerates the outbreak of insurgencies—and this is not always a blessing for the insurgents, as we have seen in the cases of the Communist movements in Asia after the 1948 Calcutta meeting—and sometimes slows them down or inhibits them entirely, when insurgencies do not fit in with the over-all policy of the Communist bloc. This last point cannot be documented, naturally, but there are strong presumptions that the surprisingly quiet attitude of the Indonesian Communist Party today, which seems powerful enough to go into violent action, may be attributed to some sort of veto from Moscow and/or Peking.

If outside support is too easily obtainable, it can destroy or harm self-reliance in the insurgent ranks. For this reason, partly, Communist insurgents in Asia have always emphasized the necessity of counting on their own efforts. The resolution of the First Session of the Vietnamese Central Committee of the Lao Dong (Communist) Party in 1951 reminded Party members that "our Resistance War is a long and hard struggle" and "we have mainly to rely on our own forces."

In conclusion, (1) a cause, (2) a police and administrative weakness in the counterinsurgent camp, (3) a not-too-hostile geographic environment, and (4) outside support in the middle and later stages of an insurgency— these are the conditions for a successful insurgency. The first two are musts. The last one is a help that may become a necessity.

NOTES

1. Buck's *Land Utilization in China* (London: Oxford University Press, 1937) was based on investigations conducted in 1929–33 in 16,786 farms, 168 localities, 154 hsien (counties), 22 provinces.

Table 22 gives the percentages of farmers who were owners, part-owners, and tenants:

Owners: 54.2%   Part-owners: 39.9%   Tenants: 5.9%

In the wheat region of North China, where the Communists were strongly established, the percentages were:

Owners: 76.1%   Part-owners: 21.8%   Tenants: 2.1%

Table 23 gives the average sizes of farms (in hectares) by class of ownership. In the wheat region:

Owners: 2.25   Part-owners: 2.25   Tenants: 2.05

Another table gives the numbers and percentages of farms in each size class. For the wheat region:

Very Small: 2   Small: 24   Medium: 34   Medium Large: 17   Large: 12
Very Large: 9   Very, Very Large: 2   Very, Very, Very Large: 0

The Chinese Communist figures on land distribution, based on a report by Liu Shao-ch'i in June, 1950, were these: "Landlords and peasants, who account for less than 10 per cent of the rural population, own 70 to 80 per cent of all the land, while poor peasants, agricultural laborers and middle peasants, who account for about 90 per cent of the rural population, own only 20 to 30 per cent of the land. . . ." (Editorial in *Jen-min Jih-Pao*, as quoted in C. K. Yang, *A Chinese Village in Early Communist Transition* [Cambridge, Mass.: The Technology Press, Massachusetts Institute of Technology, 1959].)

2. Bernard Fall, *Le Viet-Minh* (Paris: Librairie Armand Colin, 1960), p. 195.

Chapter 3

THE INSURGENCY DOCTRINE

STRATEGIC PATTERNS FOR INSURGENCY

Since counterinsurgency exists solely as a reaction to an insurgency, the counterinsurgent's problems and operations can be best understood in the light of what prompts them. In this chapter, we shall summarize the insurgency doctrine.

Two general patterns for insurgencies emerge from the history of past revolutionary wars. One is based essentially on the theory and experience of the Chinese Communists and was offered by Liu Shao-ch'i as a blueprint for revolution in colonial and semicolonial countries:

The path that led the Chinese people to victory is expressed in the following formula:

1. The working class must unite with all other classes, political parties, and organizations and individuals who are willing to oppose the oppression of imperialism and its lackeys, form a broad and nationwide united front, and wage a resolute fight against imperialism and its lackeys.
2. This nationwide united front must be led and built around the working class, which opposes imperialism most resolutely, most courageously, and most unselfishly, and its party, the Communist Party, with the latter as its center. It must not be led by the wavering and compromising national bourgeoisie or the petty bourgeoisie and its parties.
3. In order to enable the working class and its party, the Communist Party, to become the center for uniting all the forces throughout the country against imperialism and to lead the national united front competently to

victory, it is necessary to build up through long struggles a Communist Party which is armed with the theory of Marxism-Leninism, which understands strategy and tactics, practices self-criticism and strict discipline, and which is closely linked with the masses.

4. It is necessary to set up wherever and whenever possible a national army that is led by the Communist Party and is powerful and skillful in fighting the enemies. It is necessary to set up bases on which the liberation army can rely for its activities and to coordinate the mass struggles in the enemy-controlled areas with the armed struggles. Armed struggle is the main form of struggle for the national liberation struggles of many colonies and semicolonies.

This is the basic way followed and practiced in China by the Chinese people in winning victory. This is the way of Mao Tse-tung, which may also be the basic way in winning emancipation by the people of other colonial and semicolonial countries where similar conditions prevail.[1]

The other pattern, a variation of the first in its early stage, has been followed in several nationalist insurgencies.

They will be described next, but it must be understood that they are given only as patterns built on generalizations. While they substantially fit the actual events in their broad lines, they may be partially at variance with the history of specific insurgencies.

THE ORTHODOX PATTERN (COMMUNIST)

To the Communists, revolution consists not merely in overthrowing the existing order but also in carrying out afterward a complete Communist transformation of the country.

The First Step: Creation of a Party

The basic instrument for the entire process is a party, and the first step for the insurgent is to create it.

By definition, it should be the party of the proletariat, but since the proletariat is small or nonexistent in colonial and semicolonial countries, the lowest class of peasants must be included in it; inclusion of the peasants is indeed a *sine qua non,* inasmuch as the coming armed struggle has to be conducted in the rural areas. Because the proletariat cannot produce the competent early leaders, they must be sought for among the intellectuals and particularly among the students, who can provide ardor as well as brain.

The intensity, the vicissitudes of the long struggles ahead make it imperative that the party be strong, disciplined, tested. It must not be a loose organization, which may break apart at the first sharp turn in party policy or give way under the reaction of the counterinsurgent. In addition, it must not disintegrate in the aftermaths of victory, when Communist reforms are about to be implemented and when yesterday's allies become today's enemies. It must be and stay an elite party.

Its cohesion can be maintained by imposing on the members acceptance of the two basic functioning rules—democratic centralism, and criticism and self-criticism; by screening the applicants through the easy criterion of their class origin; by making the applicants' sponsors responsible for their present and future behavior.

Its purity is maintained by systematic, regular weeding-out conducted in "intra-Party struggles," which are considered as a welcome necessity by Liu Shao-ch'i. Deviators from orthodoxy are won back by conciliatory methods or expelled if they do not confess their errors.

In view of its future operations, the party must be organized into both open and clandestine apparatuses, the latter designed for a dual purpose: defensive, in case the counterinsurgent decides to suppress the party; offensive in order to subvert and to conduct the mass struggles in the enemy's areas once the party has gone into open rebellion.

It cannot be denied that the creation and the growth of such a party is at best a slow, painstaking process. In the case of the Chinese Communist Party, five years elapsed between the meeting of its 12 founders in Shanghai on July 1, 1921, and its first 1,000 members. Building a strong, reliable revolutionary party is certainly the most difficult part in the insurgency. If it were easy to achieve, the world might well be Communist by now, considering the machine, the experience, the efforts, and the money the Communist Internationale has applied to the purpose. Errors in leadership, human inertia, circumstances beyond the insurgent's control, and bad luck have provided tremendous and recurrent obstacles.

On the other hand, this first step can be accomplished by legal and peaceful means, at least in the countries where political opposition is tolerated.

The Second Step: United Front

An elite party is perforce a minority party. It cannot overpower the counterinsurgent by itself, with its own means. Therefore, the second step, which may largely overlap with the first, consists in rallying allies around the party—the more the better. This raises several problems:

A large united front will necessarily include dubious allies whose use must be curbed short of the point where they can endanger the basic program of the insurgent. The solution is "salami tactics": once the party is firmly in power, the allies no longer needed will be rejected one by one.

The party may lose its identity in a united front. In order to reduce this risk, the party must always remain a "bloc without" in any coalition. It can enter an alliance with other parties, but it must never merge with them. It cannot absorb them, either; sympathetic but unreliable elements must be grouped in the party's front organizations.

The party's platform at any given time during the conflict must contain something that appeals to each ally and nothing that may be too objectionable to them. So the real postwar intentions of the party must be kept secret; they need be disclosed only to the top leadership. If the rank and file are disciplined, they will accept a watered-down official program for the sake of tactics. When the Chinese Communists were asked about their future program, they used to reply in a convincing fashion that China was not ripe for Communist reforms, a long period of transition was necessary, China had first to pass through a period of national capitalist development. The "period of transition" actually lasted less than two years (1949–51).

During this second step, the party's clandestine apparatus will engage in subversive action directed toward three main elements:

The counterinsurgent, with a view toward preventing and sabotaging an eventual reaction.

The allies, in order to channel their activity in the direction chosen by the party and to prevent any damaging split in the united front.

The masses, in order to prepare and to promote the political struggles against the counterinsurgent.

This is done by infiltration, *noyautage,* agitation, and propaganda. Good intelligence is an important by-product of this work.

As the moment for the armed struggle approaches, the work among the masses becomes particularly important in the rural areas that have been tentatively selected as favorable grounds for the insurgent's initial military operations. A population largely won over to the cause and an area where the party organization is strong are essential for the success of the first guerrilla operations, on which much depends.

The insurgent's activity during the second step remains generally within the bounds of legality and nonviolence. It does not constitute an open rebellion, a clear-cut challenge to the counterinsurgent. Having the initiative, the insurgent can always slow down or retreat if a reaction threatens.

The Third Step: Guerrilla Warfare

The insurgent may seize power merely by political play and subversion. If not, then an armed struggle is the logical continuation. The

Chinese Communists assert that the armed struggle is both necessary and indispensable, that victory must be won by force, that "liberation" must not be granted or gained by compromise. The reasons for their stand are these:

A local revolutionary war is part of the global war against capitalism and imperialism. Hence, a military victory against the local enemy is in fact a victory against the global enemy and contributes to his ultimate defeat.

When the insurgent seizes power after an armed struggle, his victory is complete, his authority absolute. The war has polarized the population, revealing friends and enemies, which makes it easier to implement the Communist postwar program.

Through the armed struggle, the party consolidates itself. It acquires experience, once and for all cures its infantile diseases, eliminates the weak members, is able to select the best, the true leaders. The logical implication of this is that the insurgent must win primarily through his own effort; if he is put into power by external intervention, the party's internal weakness will plague him for years.

The party assumes power with a tested, reliable military establishment, which is the party's guarantor in the political transformation to come.

So, whether because it is impossible to succeed otherwise or because of his faith in the usefulness of the armed struggle, the insurgent embarks on a contest of strength. The decision being his,[2] he chooses the time when conditions seem ripe, when, *internally*, the counterinsurgent is weakened by a fortuitous or provoked crisis, when subversion is producing effects, when public opinion is divided, when the party's organization has been built up in some rural areas; and when, *externally*, direct intervention on the counterinsurgent's side is unlikely, when the insurgent can count on some moral and political support at this stage and on military aid later, if necessary.

The goal is the creation of the insurgent's military power, but it has to be accomplished progressively, step by step. Guerrilla warfare is the only possible course of action for a start. In this step, the first objective is the guerrilla's survival: the final one, the acquisition of bases in which an insurgent government and administration will be established, the human and other resources exploited, and regular forces created. Guerrilla warfare with no bases, says Mao Tse-tung, is nothing but roving banditism; unable to maintain links with the population, it cannot develop and is bound to be defeated.

Objectively, there is no difference between ordinary, everyday bandit activity in almost every country and the first guerrilla actions. What makes it possible for the guerrillas to survive and to expand? The complicity of the population. This is the key to guerrilla warfare, indeed to the insurgency, and it has been expressed in the formula of the fish swimming in the water. The complicity of the population is not to be confused with the sympathy of the population; the former is active, the latter inactive, and the popularity of the insurgent's cause is insufficient by itself to transform sympathy into complicity. The participation of the population in the conflict is obtained, above all, by a political organization (the party) living among the population, backed by force (the guerrilla gangs), which eliminates the open enemies, intimidates the potential ones, and relies on those among the population who actively support the insurgents. Persuasion brings a minority of supporters—they are indispensable—but force rallies the rest. There is, of course, a practical if not ethical limit to the use of force; the basic rule is never to antagonize at any one time more people than can be handled.

Just as important as the links between the insurgent's political organization and the population are the links between his armed forces and the masses. To see that they are properly maintained—and that the forces never become a rival to the party—is the task of the political commissars.

The guerrilla operations will be planned primarily not so much against the counterinsurgent as in order to organize the population. An ambush against a counterinsurgent patrol may be a military success, but if it does not bring the support of a village or implicate its population against the counterinsurgent, it is not a victory because it does not lead to expansion. In other words, attrition of the enemy is a by-product of guerrilla warfare, not its essential goal.

Where to operate? In the areas that the counterinsurgent cannot easily control and where the guerrilla gangs can consequently survive and develop. The factors in selecting the first areas of operations are:

The strength of the insurgent's organization among the population that has been achieved in preliminary work.

The remoteness of the areas from the center of the counterinsurgent's power.

Their inaccessibility due to terrain and poor communications.

Their location on both sides of administrative borders, which makes it difficult for the enemy to coordinate his reaction.

Later on, as success breeds success, the first factor becomes less important, and guerrilla warfare can be expanded geographically by injecting teams of guerrilla units and political workers in other areas, even if they are devoid of strong party structures. This underlines the importance of early success.

Armament is not a problem at this stage. The insurgent's requirements are small. Weapons (pistols, rifles, shotguns) are generally available or can be bought and smuggled in. Crude weapons (grenades, mines, even mortars) can be manufactured, and equipment can be captured from the enemy.

Demoralization of the enemy's forces is an important task. The most effective way to achieve it is by employing a policy of leniency toward the prisoners. They must be well treated and offered the choice of joining the movement or of being set free, even if this means that they will return to the counterinsurgent's side. Despite its setbacks in the early stages, this is the policy that pays the most in the long run. During a trip in western China in April, 1947, the author was captured by Communist troops under General Ch'en Keng in Hsinkiang, a town in Shansi Province. He was treated as a prisoner the first morning, put under surveillance for the rest of the day, and considered as a "guest of honor" for his week-long involuntary but highly interesting stay among the People's Liberation Army. During this week, various military and political cadres undertook to explain their policy, strategy, and tactics. A political commissar explained the Communist technique for handling Kuomintang prisoners. They were offered the choice between (1) joining the Communist Army, (2) settling in Communist territory, where they would be given a share of land, (3) going back home, or (4) returning to the Nationalist Army. A few days later, the author visited a temporary prisoner camp where the Communists were keeping a group of 200 junior Nationalist officers who had just been captured. While the political commissar was busy talking to a group of prisoners, the author asked another group, in Chinese, whether any among them had previously been captured by the Communists. Three Nationalist officers admitted this was their second capture.

In that same month, a colleague of the author visited a camp at Hsuchow in central China, where the Nationalists kept 5,000 Communist prisoners.

"Where were they caught?" he asked the Nationalist general in charge of the camp.

"Between you and me, we have no more than ten real Communist soldiers among these prisoners."

"Who are the others then?"

"Nationalist soldiers caught and released by the Communists. We don't want them to contaminate our army."

Thus, the Communists had achieved the trick of having the Nationalists themselves watching their own men! The Chinese Communists first used this technique with surprising success on Japanese prisoners during the Sino-Japanese War. In the early postwar period, several important Japanese Communist leaders were graduates of the Chinese school for Japanese prisoners. The first clear sign of the Chinese influence on the Vietminh came in 1950, when the Vietminh suddenly changed their attitude toward French prisoners. Instead of slaughtering them, they undertook to brainwash them.

In addition to the foregoing matters of supply and operations, the insurgent must solve a problem created by what we have considered a tactical asset: the scattered nature of his operations. Although this makes it difficult for the counterinsurgent to cope with them, the insurgent must also reconcile the dilution of his forces with the need for unity of action. The solution is a clear, common doctrine widely taught and accepted.

The united-front policy remains in force throughout the conflict and must be given substance during the armed struggle. How can allies be admitted into the political structures and the guerrilla units without weakening the insurgency? The only way is by confronting the allies with the party's superiority in organization, discipline, doctrine, policy, leadership. The party alone must lead; forceful leaders among the allies must be won over or neutralized. The party alone must expand; the allied parties may be permitted only to stagnate.

The military tactics of guerrilla warfare are too well known to be elaborated upon in this summary.

The Fourth Step: Movement Warfare

Guerrilla warfare cannot win the decision against a resolute enemy. Protracted guerrilla activity, so cheap to carry out and so expensive to suppress, may eventually produce a crisis in the counterinsurgent camp, but it could just as well alienate the population and disintegrate the united front. The enemy must be met on his own ground; an insurgent regular army has to be created in order to destroy the counterinsurgent forces.

There is a problem of timing. If premature, the creation of this regular army, which necessarily is less elusive than guerrilla gangs, may lead to disaster. So it must not be undertaken until bases have been liberated and the enemy discouraged from invading them too frequently, and until the problem of armament is likely to be solved.

When the situation fulfills these conditions the best guerrilla units can be progressively transformed into regular troops, first of company strength, then of battalion strength, and so on up to division level or even higher.

Armament is the foremost difficulty. The amount and the type of weapons and equipment available set the limit for the expansion of the insurgent's regular forces. Production in the bases cannot be counted upon because the arsenals offer fixed and easy targets for the counterinsurgent.

This leaves two possible sources: capture from the enemy and supply from abroad.

Of these, it is capture from the enemy that dictates the nature of the insurgent's operations. They will be "commercial operations," conceived and executed in order to bring more gains than losses.[3] This, in turn, requires an overwhelming and sudden concentration of insurgent forces against an isolated counterinsurgent unit caught in the open—not entrenched; hence a *movement warfare* in which the insurgent can exploit his fluidity, his better intelligence, and the simple but effective cross-country logistical facilities afforded by the organized population. For the sake of fluidity, heavy armament must be ruled out; because of the limited logistical facilities, the actual shock must be brief, and no sustained attack can be undertaken; for the sake of better intelligence, operations are preferably conducted in areas where the insurgent political organizations are strong and active among the population.

Supply from abroad, if such a possibility exists, imposes on the insurgent the necessity of acquiring bases on or near the international border of the country, close to the source of supply.

The insurgent units' lack of punch—their feeble logistical capacities—rule out fixed defensive operations. In fact, so precious are the regular units, particularly when they have just been created, that the defense of the bases has to be left to other insurgent forces, to the population itself with its militias, to the guerrilla units, and to the local troops, which provide a core for the defense. In offensive operations, these second-rate units will also relieve the regular troops from the task of covering and reconnoitering.

The territorial pattern of the insurgent's strategy is reflected in the various types of areas he sets up:

Regular bases, areas garrisoned by regular troops (at rest, in training, or in the process of being organized) and local troops, with an openly functioning government carrying out administration, economic policy, taxation, justice, education, and public services, safe from enemy penetration unless the counterinsurgent mobilizes forces from other parts of the country for a major campaign.

Guerrilla bases, with active regular troops in addition to the other types, fully organized under the insurgent's political control, with administrative organs devised to function either openly or underground, as circumstances dictate. They are subject to more frequent enemy penetrations, but the enemy is generally unable to remain in them.

Guerrilla areas, where the counterinsurgent forces and governments are constantly contending with the insurgent's.

Occupied areas, under the counterinsurgent's political and military control, where the insurgent works only underground.

The aim of the insurgent is to change the occupied areas into guerrilla areas, guerrilla areas into guerrilla bases, and these into regular bases.

In order to mobilize the population for a total war effort, every inhabitant under the insurgent's control is made to belong simultaneously to at least two organizations: one, *horizontal,* is a geographic organization, by hamlet, village, or district; the other, *vertical,* groups the inhabitants by categories of every kind, by age, by sex, by profession. The party cells crisscross the whole structure and provide the cement. An additional organization helps to keep everybody in line: the party's secret service, whose members remain unknown to the local cadres and answer only to the top hierarchy, which is thus in a position to control those who control the masses. In 1947, when the author was captured by the Chinese Communists in Hsinkiang, in Shansi Province, he noticed that a team of Communist civil servants immediately took over the administration of the town, which was the seat of a *hsien* (county). These officials, he was told, had long before been designated for the task and had been functioning as a shadow government with the guerrilla units active in the area.

"Your forces are not going to occupy Hsinkiang permanently. What will happen to your civil officials when your army leaves?" I asked the political commissar of General Ch'en Keng's army.

"They will leave, too, and resume their clandestine work," he replied.

"Are you not afraid that they will lose their value now that they have revealed themselves?"

"We have secret agents in this town who did not come out when we took it. We don't even know who they are. They will still be here when we go."

The expansion of the insurgent movement raises the problem of political and military cadres. They are selected on the basis, above all, of their loyalty and, secondly, of their concrete achievements in the field. How important the Communists consider the loyalty of their personnel, cadres, and troops can be seen from the following story. In 1952, a Vietminh regimental commander, hard pressed by French troops in the Red River Delta, pleaded for replacements. The answer from the Vietminh command: "Impossible to send you replacements now; they have not yet received full political indoctrination."

The Communist officers, both Chinese and Vietminh, were the product of natural selection. They had shown their mettle in the field before they were selected for higher responsibilities. Theoretical studies and postgraduate work in the next higher echelon completed their education. Compare the Communist products with the officers in the South Vietnamese Army today—picked according to academic standards and, therefore, generally sons of urban petty bourgeois. They are just as alien to, and lost in, the paddy fields as the white officers are, and possibly less adaptable.

The Fifth Step: Annihilation Campaign

As the over-all strength of the insurgent grows while his opponent's decreases, a balance of forces is reached at some point. In the assessment of the insurgent's strength must be included not only his military assets but the solidity of his political structure, the fact that the population is mobilized in his areas, the subversive activity of his underground agents in the counterinsurgent's areas, and finally, the insurgent's psychological superiority.

From then on, the scope and scale of the insurgent's operations will increase swiftly; a series of offensives aiming at the complete destruction of the enemy will constitute the last and final step.

At any time during the process, the insurgent may make peace offers, provided there is more to gain by negotiating than by fighting.

THE BOURGEOIS-NATIONALIST PATTERN: A SHORTCUT

The goal of the insurgent in this case is generally limited to the seizure of power; postinsurgency problems, as secondary preoccupations, are shelved for the time being. The precise and immediate aim of the initial core of insurgents, a dedicated but inevitably small group of men with no broad organization to back them, is to set up a revolutionary party rapidly.

The First Step: Blind Terrorism

The purpose is to get publicity for the movement and its cause, and by focusing attention on it, to attract latent supporters. This is done by random terrorism, bombings, arson, assassinations, conducted in as spectacular a fashion as possible, by concentrated, coordinated, and synchronized waves. Few men are needed for this sort of operation. According to Mohamed Boudiaf, one of the early FLN leaders, no more than 400 or 500 Algerian Nationalists took part in the terrorist actions on D day.

The hijacking of a Portuguese ship by an opponent of Premier Salazar, the temporary abduction of a world-famous racing-car champion by Castro's men in Havana had no purpose other than to attract headlines.

The Second Step: Selective Terrorism

This quickly follows the first. The aims are to isolate the counterinsurgent from the masses, to involve the population in the struggle, and to obtain as a minimum its passive complicity.

This is done by killing, in various parts of the country, some of the low-ranking government officials who work most closely with the population, such as policemen, mailmen, mayors, councilmen, and teachers. Killing high-ranking counterinsurgent officials serves no purpose since they are too far removed from the population for their deaths to serve as examples.

The early supporters are set to work collecting money from the population. Although money, the sinew of war, is interesting in itself, this operation has important side effects. The amount of money collected provides a simple standard to gauge the efficiency of the supporters and to select leaders accordingly. It also implicates the mass and forces it to show its revolutionary spirit. "You give money, you are with us. You refuse money, you are a traitor." A few of those unwilling to pay are executed. In order to involve the population further, simple *mots d'ordres* are circulated, such as "boycott tobacco"; a few violators caught smoking are executed. These assassinations have value only if they serve as examples; therefore they must not be hidden or committed on the sly. The victims are generally found with a tag explaining that they have been condemned by a revolutionary tribunal and executed for such and such a crime.

The insurgent has to destroy all bridges linking the population with the counterinsurgent and his potential allies. Among these, people (generally the liberal-minded) inclined to seek a compromise with the insurgents will be targets of terrorist attacks.

When all this is achieved, conditions are ripe for the insurgent guerrillas to operate and for the population to be mobilized effectively. From there on, this pattern rejoins the orthodox one, if necessary.

Illegal and violent at the outset, dangerous for the insurgent because terrorism may backfire, this pattern may save years of tedious organizational work. By terrorism, small groups of insurgents have been catapulted overnight to the top of large revolutionary movements, and some have won their victory at that very time, without need for further action. However, the bill is paid at the end with the bitterness bred by terrorism and with the usual postvictory disintegration of a party hastily thrown together.

VULNERABILITY OF THE INSURGENT IN THE ORTHODOX PATTERN

Let us follow the insurgent who has selected the orthodox pattern as his course of action. He operates necessarily in a country where political opposition is tolerated.

During the first two steps—creation of a party and organization of a united front—his vulnerability depends directly on the tolerance of the counterinsurgent and can be correspondingly low or high. Sooner or later, the counterinsurgent realizes the danger and starts reacting. The insurgent's vulnerability rises because he has not yet acquired military power and is in no position to resist by force. if the counterinsurgent's reaction is feeble enough, the insurgent has survived his first test, has learned how far he can go, and his vulnerability decreases.

If all has proceeded well, the insurgent has created his party and organized a popular front. He decides now to initiate a guerrilla warfare (Step 3). His military power is still nil or feeble, whereas the full weight of his opponent's may be brought to bear against him. Consequently, the insurgent's vulnerability rises sharply to its highest level, and he may well be destroyed. If he survives, his vulnerability goes down again until he starts

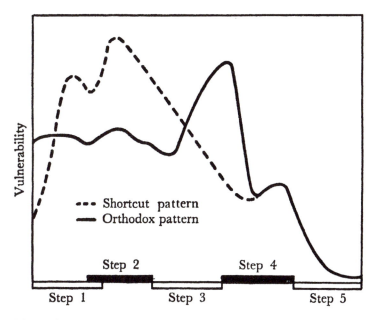

Figure 3. Vulnerability of the Insurgent in the Course of the Revolutionary War

organizing a regular army (Step 4): His units, no longer small, elusive guerrilla groups, then offer better targets for the counterinsurgent's conventional forces. Vulnerability increases once more. After this last hurdle is cleared, the insurgent is no longer vulnerable.

If vulnerability could be measured, it might be graphically represented as shown in Figure 3.

VULNERABILITY OF THE INSURGENT IN THE SHORTCUT PATTERN

In the case when the insurgent has chosen to follow the bourgeois-nationalist pattern, his vulnerability starts from a lower level since his action is clandestine at the outset. It climbs rapidly because of the danger inherent in terrorism, which the normal police force may be able to suppress if it has not been planned and conducted on a sufficient scale. The insurgent, who needs publicity above everything else at this stage, is also at the mercy of a tight and prompt censorship.

However, surprise plays in his favor, and he can count on the fact that the counterinsurgent's reaction is never immediate. If the insurgent has survived the first few days of blind terrorism, his vulnerability decreases.

It soon rises again because the full power of the counterinsurgent begins to be mobilized against him; the armed forces, particularly, go into action much sooner than in the orthodox pattern. Vulnerability goes up to a new height. If the insurgent survives, it diminishes progressively.

When the insurgent reaches Step 3 (guerrilla warfare) and rejoins the orthodox pattern, he is less vulnerable than he would have been had he chosen the orthodox pattern at the start because he has already successfully withstood the full brunt of the counterinsurgent reaction.

NOTES

1. Address at the Trade-Union Conference of Asian and Australasian Countries, Peking, November, 1949. The colonial and semicolonial countries comprise all Asia (with the exception of the Communist states), all Africa, and all Latin America. (See maps, pp. 140 and 142.)

2. With the reservation expressed on p. 6: A Communist insurgent movement may be ordered by the Communist International to step up or to slow down its action.

3. Trying to chew off too much too soon was the mistake made by General Giap in Tonkin in 1951, when he attempted to force a showdown with the French forces under General de Lattre de Tassigny. The result was a costly defeat for the insurgents.

Chapter 4

COUNTERINSURGENCY IN THE COLD REVOLUTIONARY WAR

From the counterinsurgent's point of view, a revolutionary war can be divided into two periods:

1. The "cold revolutionary war," when the insurgent's activity remains on the whole legal and nonviolent (as in Steps 1 and 2 in the orthodox pattern).
2. The "hot revolutionary war," when the insurgent's activity becomes openly illegal and violent (as in the other steps in the orthodox pattern and in the entire process of the shortcut pattern).

The transitions from "peace" to "war," as we have seen, can be very gradual and confusing. Even when the insurgent follows the shortcut pattern, violence is always preceded by a short period of stirrings. In Algeria, for instance, the police, the administration, and the government suspected that something was brewing during the summer of 1954. For analytical purposes, we shall choose as a dividing line between the two periods the moment when the counterinsurgent armed forces are ordered to step in, and we shall approach the study of counterinsurgency warfare in chronological order, starting with the "cold revolutionary war."

The situation at this stage is characterized by the fact that the insurgent operates largely on the legal side, and only partly on the fringe of legality, through his subversion tactics. He may or may not have been recognized as an insurgent; if he has been identified as such, only the police and a few people in the government generally realize what is looming.

The essential problem for the counterinsurgent stems from the fact that the actual danger will always appear to the nation as out of proportion to the demands made by an adequate response. The potential danger is enormous, but how to prove it on the basis of available, objective facts? How to justify the efforts and sacrifices needed to smother the incipient insurgency? The insurgent, if he knows how to conduct his war, is banking on precisely this situation, and will see to it that the transition from peace to war is very gradual indeed. The case of Algeria gives an excellent illustration of the counterinsurgent's dilemma because the insurgent made an effort to start with a big "bang," and yet the dilemma persisted. The Algerian rebels, with publicity foremost in their minds, set November 1, 1954, as their D day. Seventy separate actions took place, scattered all over the territory—bomb throwings, assassinations, sabotage, minor harassments of isolated military posts—all largely ineffectual. And then nothing. According to Mohamed Boudiaf, one of the chief planners of the insurgency, the results were "disastrous in a large part of Algeria. In the Oran region, notably, the repression was extremely brutal and efficient. . . . It was impossible for me during the first two months even to establish a liaison between the Rif [in Spanish Morocco] and the Oran region."[1] Was it enough to warrant a mobilization of French resources and energy, a disruption of the economy, the imposition of a war status on the country?

Four general courses of action are open to the counterinsurgent under these circumstances, and they are not mutually exclusive:

1. He may act directly on the insurgent leaders.
2. He may act indirectly on the conditions that are propitious to an insurgency.
3. He may infiltrate the insurgent movement and try to make it ineffective.
4. He may build up or reinforce his political machine.

DIRECT ACTION AGAINST THE INSURGENT

The direct approach consists of depriving the insurgent of any physical possibility of building up his movement. At this stage, the insurgent's movement generally has no life of its own; everything depends on its leaders, who are, consequently, the key elements. By arresting them or by restricting their ability to contact people, by impeaching them in the courts, by banning their organizations and publications if necessary, the counterinsurgent may nip the insurgency in the bud.

Such a method is easy, of course, in totalitarian countries, but it is hardly feasible in democracies. One of two situations may arise: Either the counterinsurgent government may already have equipped itself as a precautionary measure (even in the absence of pressure) with special powers and laws designed to cope with insurgencies. In this case, the main problem is to act without giving undue publicity to the insurgent, an important matter particularly if the insurgent's cause has a wide popular appeal.

The other possibility is that the counterinsurgent may not have provided himself in advance with the necessary powers. Thus when he attempts to act directly against the insurgent, he opens a Pandora's box. Arrests have to be justified. On what basis? Where is the limit to be drawn between normal political opposition, on the one hand, and subversion, which is difficult to define under the best circumstances? The arrested insurgent can count almost automatically on some support from the legitimate opposition parties and groups. Referred to the courts, he will take refuge in chicanery, exploit to the utmost every advantage provided by the existing laws. Worse yet, the trial itself will serve as a sounding board for his cause. The banned organizations will spring up again under other labels, and the counterinsurgent will bear the onus of proving their ties to the old ones.

The counterinsurgent will inevitably be impelled to amend normal procedures, but this time under pressure. The difficulty can be assessed easily when one recalls that it took some ten years in the United States to ban the Communist Party, which did not even have any significant appeal to the population. (Some contend, and they have a point, that it would have taken less time had the Party actually appeared dangerous.)

Since legal changes are slow, the counterinsurgent may be tempted to go a step further and to act beyond the borders of legality. A succession of arbitrary restrictive measures will be started, the nation will soon find itself under constraint, opposition will increase, and the insurgent will thank his opponent for having played into his hands.

It can be therefore concluded with relative safety that the direct approach works well if:

1. The insurgent's cause has little appeal (but we have assumed that no wise insurgent would launch an insurgency unless the prerequisite of a good cause had been fulfilled).
2. The counterinsurgent has the legal power to act.
3. The counterinsurgent can prevent the insurgent from gaining publicity.

INDIRECT ACTION AGAINST THE INSURGENT

We have seen in Chapter 2 that insurgency cannot normally develop unless two essential prerequisites are met: the insurgent's having a cause, and his being helped initially by the weakness of his opponent. Two other conditions, although not absolutely necessary, are also helpful to the insurgent: geographic factors, and outside support. By acting on these conditions, a counterinsurgent could hope to frustrate the growth of an insurgent movement.

Geographic factors are what they are and cannot be significantly changed or influenced except by displacing the population—an absurdity in peacetime—or by building artificial fences, which is also too costly in peacetime. The question of outside support offers more leeway but rests largely outside the counterinsurgent's reach.

To deprive the insurgent of a good cause amounts to solving the country's basic problems. If this is possible, well and good, but we know now that a good cause for the insurgent is one that his opponent cannot adopt without losing his power in the process. And there are problems that, although providing a good cause to an insurgent, are not susceptible of solution. Is there an intelligent solution to the racial problem in South Africa? It will continue to exist as long as two different races continue to live in the same territory.

Alleviating the weaknesses in the counterinsurgent's rule seems more promising. Adapting the judicial system to the threat, strengthening the bureaucracy, reinforcing the police and the armed forces may discourage insurgency attempts, if the counterinsurgent leadership is resolute and vigilant.

INFILTRATION OF THE INSURGENT MOVEMENT

An insurgent movement in its infancy is necessarily small; hence, the views and attitudes of its members have a greater importance at the early period than at any other time. They are all, so to speak, generals with no privates to command. History is full of cases of obscure political movements that floundered and vanished soon after they were created because the founders did not agree and split the movement.

A young insurgent movement is necessarily inexperienced and should be relatively easy to infiltrate with agents who will help to disintegrate it from within and to derail it. If they do not succeed in this, they can at least report its activity.

Two famous cases of infiltration may be mentioned. In Czarist Russia, the Okhrana had succeeded in infiltrating the Bolshevik Party to such an extent and with such zeal that it was sometimes difficult to tell whether the agents were acting as Bolsheviks or as agents. A Grand Duke was assassinated in a provocation engineered by the Okhrana. When the triumphant Bolsheviks seized the Okhrana record, Lenin discovered that some of his most trusted companions had been in the pay of the Czar's police.

This attempt was ultimately unsuccessful, but another case has shown better results so far. It is well known that the American Communist Party has been so infiltrated by the FBI as to have become innocuous.

There is much merit in this idea, but it should be remembered that the longer the insurgent movement lasts, the better will be its chances to survive its infantile diseases and to take root. It may of course dwindle by itself, without outside intervention. Relying on luck, however, does not constitute a policy.

STRENGTHENING THE POLITICAL MACHINE

Most of the counterinsurgent's efforts in the "hot" revolutionary war, as we shall show, tend to build a political machine at the grass roots in order to isolate the insurgent from the population forever.

This strategy, on which we shall not elaborate now, is just as valid in the cold revolutionary war, and it should be easier to implement preventively than when the insurgent has already seized control of the population. Such a strategy, to us, represents the principal course of action for the counterinsurgent because it leaves the least to chance and makes full use of the counterinsurgent's possibilities.

It may be useful to remember that a peacetime political machine is built essentially on patronage.

NOTE

1. *Le Monde* (Paris), November 2, 1962.

Chapter 5

COUNTERINSURGENCY IN THE HOT REVOLUTIONARY WAR

Force, when it comes into play in a revolutionary war, has the singular virtue of clearing away many difficulties for the counterinsurgent, notably the matter of the issue. The moral fog dissipates sooner or later, the enemy stands out more conspicuously, repressive measures are easier to justify. But force adds, of course, its own difficulties.

At our point of departure in the study of the hot revolutionary war—that is, the moment when the armed forces have been ordered to step in—the situation usually conforms to the following pattern:

The insurgent has succeeded in building his political organization. He directs either an elite party leading a united front, or a large revolutionary movement bound to the cause. Although his actions other than subversion are overt, he operates clandestinely.

The country's map reveals three sorts of areas:

The "red" areas, where the insurgent effectively controls the population and carries out guerrilla warfare.

The "pink" areas, in which he attempts to expand; there are some efforts at organizing the populations and some guerrilla activity.

The "white" areas, not yet affected but nevertheless threatened; they are subjected to the insurgent's subversion but all seems quiet.

Confusion is prevalent in the counterinsurgent's camp. There is a realization that an emergency exists, but the feeling of crisis is more widely spread in government circles than among the population of the white and even the pink areas. The true allegiance of every citizen is open to doubt. The leadership and its policy are questioned. The political, the judicial, the military structures geared for ordinary days have not yet been adapted to the requirements of the situation. The economy is rapidly deteriorating; the government's expenses are rising while its income is declining. In the psychological field, the insurgent has the edge since he exploits a cause without which he would not have been able to develop so far as to engage in guerrilla warfare or terrorism. The counterinsurgent forces are torn between the necessity of guarding key areas and fixed installations, of protecting lives and property, and the urge to track the insurgent forces.

With this general picture in mind, we shall now discuss the various avenues open to the counterinsurgent.

LAWS AND PRINCIPLES OF COUNTERINSURGENCY WARFARE

Limits of Conventional Warfare

Let us assume that the political and economic difficulties have been magically solved or have proved manageable,[1] and that only one problem remains, the military one—how to suppress the insurgent forces. It is not a problem of means since the counterinsurgent forces are still largely superior to the insurgent's, even though they may be dispersed. It is primarily a problem of strategy and tactics, of methods and organization.

The strategy of conventional warfare prescribes the conquest of the enemy's territory, the destruction of his forces. The trouble here is that the enemy holds no territory and refuses to fight for it. He is everywhere and nowhere. By concentrating sufficient forces, the counterinsurgent can at any time penetrate and garrison a red area. Such an operation, if well sustained, may reduce guerrilla activity, but if the situation becomes untenable for the guerrillas, they will transfer their activity to another area and the problem remains unsolved. It many even be aggravated if the counterinsurgent's concentration was made at too great risk for the other areas.

The destruction of the insurgent forces requires that they be localized and immediately encircled. But they are too small to be spotted easily by the counterinsurgent's direct means of observation. Intelligence is the principal source of information on guerrillas, and intelligence has to come from the population, but the population will not talk unless it feels safe, and it does not feel safe until the insurgent's power has been broken.

The insurgent forces are also too mobile to be encircled and annihilated easily. If the counterinsurgent, on receiving news that guerrillas have been spotted, uses his ready forces immediately, chances are they will be too small for the task. If he gathers larger forces, he will have lost time and probably the benefit of surprise.

True, modern means of transportation—particularly helicopters, when available—allow the counterinsurgent to combine strength with swiftness. True, systematic large-scale operations, because of their very size, alleviate somewhat the intelligence and mobility deficiency of the counterinsurgent. Nevertheless, conventional operations by themselves have at best no more effect than a fly swatter. Some guerrillas are bound to be caught, but new recruits will replace them as fast as they are lost. If the counterinsurgent operations are sustained over a period of months, the guerrilla losses may not be so easily replaced. The question is, can the counterinsurgent operations be so sustained?

It the counterinsurgent is so strong as to be able to saturate the entire country with garrisons, military operations along conventional lines will, of course, work. The insurgent, unable to grow beyond a certain level, will slowly wither away. But saturation can seldom be afforded.

Why Insurgency Warfare Does Not Work for the Counterinsurgent

Insurgency warfare is specifically designed to allow the camp afflicted with congenital weakness to acquire strength progressively while fighting. The counterinsurgent is endowed with congenital strength; for him to adopt the insurgent's warfare would be the same as for a giant to try to fit into a dwarf's clothing. How, against whom, for instance, could he use his enemy's tactics? He alone offers targets for guerrilla operations. Were he to operate as a guerrilla, he would have to have the effective support of the population guaranteed by his own political organization among the masses; if so, then the insurgent would not have it and consequently could not exist; there would be no need for the counterinsurgent's guerrilla operations. This is not to say that there is no place in counterinsurgency warfare for small commando-type operations. They cannot, however, represent the main form of the counterinsurgent's warfare.

Is it possible for the counterinsurgent to organize a clandestine force able to defeat the insurgent on his own terms? Clandestinity seems to be another of those obligations-turned-into-assets of the insurgent. How could the counterinsurgent, whose strength derives precisely from his open physical assets, build up a clandestine force except as a minor and secondary adjunct? Furthermore, room for clandestine organizations is very limited in revolutionary war. Experience shows that no rival—not to speak of hostile—clandestine movements can coexist for long; one is always absorbed by the other. The Chinese Communist maquis succeeded in suppressing almost entirely their Nationalist counterparts in the Japanese-occupied areas of north and central China. Later on, during the final round of the revolutionary war in China, ordinary bandits (almost a regular and codified profession in some parts of China) disappeared as soon as Communist guerrillas came. Tito eliminated Mikhailovitch. If the Greek Communist ELAS did not eliminate the Nationalist resistance groups, it was due to the restraint they had to show since they were entirely dependent on the Western Allies' support. More recently, the FLN in Algeria eliminated, for all practical purposes, the rival and older MNA group. Because the insurgent has first occupied the available room, attempts to introduce another clandestine movement have little chance to succeed.

Can the counterinsurgent use terrorism too? It would be self-defeating since terrorism is a source of disorder, which is precisely what the counterinsurgent aims to stop.

If conventional warfare does not work, if insurgency warfare cannot work, the inescapable conclusion is that the counterinsurgent must apply a warfare of his own that takes into account not only the nature and characteristics of the revolutionary war, but also the laws that are peculiar to counterinsurgency and the principles deriving from them.

The First Law: The Support of the Population Is as Necessary for the Counterinsurgent as for the Insurgent

What is the crux of the problem for the counterinsurgent? It is not how to clean an area. We have seen that he can always concentrate enough forces to do it, even if he has to take some risk in order to achieve the necessary concentration. The problem is, how to keep an area clean so that the counterinsurgent forces will be free to operate elsewhere.

This can be achieved only with the support of the population. If it is relatively easy to disperse and to expel the insurgent forces from a given area by purely military action, if it is possible to destroy the insurgent political organizations by intensive police action, it is impossible to prevent the return of the guerrilla units and the rebuilding of the political cells unless the population cooperates.

The population, therefore, becomes the objective for the counterinsurgent as it was for his enemy. Its tacit support, its submission to law and order, its consensus—taken for granted in normal times—have been undermined by the insurgent's activity. And the truth is that the insurgent, with his organization at the grass roots, is tactically the strongest of opponents where it counts, at the population level.

This is where the fight has to be conducted, in spite of the counterinsurgent's ideological handicap and in spite of the head start gained by the insurgent in organizing the population.

The Second Law: Support Is Gained Through an Active Minority

The original problem becomes now: how to obtain the support of the population—support not only in the form of sympathy and approval but also in active participation in the fight against the insurgent.

The answer lies in the following proposition, which simply expresses the basic tenet of the exercise of political power:

In any situation, whatever the cause, there will be an active minority for the cause, a neutral majority, and an active minority against the cause.

The technique of power consists in relying on the favorable minority in order to rally the neutral majority and to neutralize or eliminate the hostile minority.

In extreme cases, when the cause and the circumstances are extraordinarily good or bad, one of the minorities disappears or becomes negligible, and there may even be a solid unanimity for or against among the population. But such cases are obviously rare.

This holds true for every political regime, from the harshest dictatorship to the mildest democracy. What varies is the degree and the purpose to which it is applied. Mores and the constitution may impose limitations, the purpose may be good or bad, but the law remains essentially valid whatever the variations, and they can indeed be great, for the law is applied unconsciously in most countries.

It can no longer be ignored or applied unconsciously in a country beset by a revolutionary war, when what is at stake is precisely the counterinsurgent's power directly challenged by an active minority through the use of subversion and force. The counterinsurgent who refuses to use this law for his own purposes, who is bound by its peacetime limitations, tends to drag the war out without getting closer to victory.

How far to extend the limitations is a matter of ethics, and a very serious one, but no more so than bombing the civilian population in a conventional war. All wars are cruel, the revolutionary war perhaps most of all because every citizen, whatever his wish, is or will be directly and actively involved in it by the insurgent who needs him and cannot afford to let him remain neutral. The cruelty of the revolutionary war is not a mass, anonymous cruelty but a highly personalized, individual one. No greater crime can be committed by the counterinsurgent than accepting, or resigning himself to, the protraction of the war. He would do as well to give up early.

The strategic problem of the counterinsurgent may be defined now as follows: "To find the favorable minority, to organize it in order to mobilize the population against the insurgent minority." Every operation, whether in the military field or in the political, social, economic, and psychological fields, must be geared to that end.

To be sure, the better the cause and the situation, the larger will be the active minority favorable to the counterinsurgent and the easier its task. This truism dictates the main goal of the propaganda—to show that the cause and the situation of the counterinsurgent are better than the insurgent's. More important, it underlines the necessity for the counterinsurgent to come out with an acceptable countercause.

Victory in Counterinsurgency Warfare

We can now define negatively and positively what is a victory for the counterinsurgent.

A victory is not the destruction in a given area of the insurgent's forces and his political organization. If one is destroyed, it will be locally re-created by the other; if both are destroyed, they will both be re-created by a new fusion of insurgents from the outside. A negative example: the numerous mopping-up operations by the French in the Plain of Reeds in Cochinchina all through the Indochina War.

A victory is that plus the permanent isolation of the insurgent from the population, isolation not enforced upon the population but maintained by and with the population. A positive example: the defeat of the FLN in the Oran region in Algeria in 1959–60. In this region, which covers at least a third of the Algerian territory, FLN actions—counting everything from a grenade thrown in a café to cutting a telephone pole—had dwindled to an average of two a day.

Such a victory may be indirect; it is nonetheless decisive (unless of course, as in Algeria, the political goal of the counterinsurgent government changes).

The Third Law: Support from the Population Is Conditional

Once the insurgent has established his hold over the population, the minority that was hostile to him becomes invisible. Some of its members have been eliminated physically, thereby providing an example to the others; others have escaped abroad; most have been cowed into hiding their true feelings and have thus melted within the majority of the population; a few are even making a show of their support for the insurgency. The population, watched by the active supporters of the insurgency, lives under the threat of denunciation to the political cells and prompt punishment by the guerrilla units.

The minority hostile to the insurgent will not and cannot emerge as long as the threat has not been lifted to a reasonable extent. Furthermore, even after the threat has been lifted, the emerging counterinsurgent supporters will not be able to rally the bulk of the population so long as the population is not convinced that the counterinsurgent has the will, the means, and the ability to win. When a man's life is at stake, it takes more than propaganda to budge him.

Four deductions can be made from this law. Effective political action on the population must be preceded by military and police operations against the guerrilla units and the insurgent political organizations.

Political, social, economic, and other reforms, however much they ought to be wanted and popular, are inoperative when offered while the insurgent still controls the population. An attempt at land reform in Algeria in 1957 fell flat when the FLN assassinated some Moslem peasants who had received land.

The counterinsurgent needs a convincing success as early as possible in order to demonstrate that he has the will, the means, and the ability to win.

The counterinsurgent cannot safely enter into negotiations except from a position of strength, or his potential supporters will flock to the insurgent side.

In conventional warfare, strength is assessed according to military or other tangible criteria, such as the number of divisions, the position they hold, the industrial resources, etc. In revolutionary warfare, strength must be assessed by the extent of support from the population as measured in terms of political organization at the grass roots. The counterinsurgent reaches a position of strength when his power is embodied in a political organization issuing from, and firmly supported by, the population.

The Fourth Law: Intensity of Efforts and Vastness of Means Are Essential

The operations needed to relieve the population from the insurgent's threat and to convince it that the counterinsurgent will ultimately win are necessarily of an intensive nature and of long duration. They require a large concentration of efforts, resources, and personnel.

This means that the efforts cannot be diluted all over the country but must be applied successively area by area.

STRATEGY OF THE COUNTERINSURGENCY

Translated into a general strategy, the principles derived from these few laws suggest the following step-by-step procedure:

In a Selected Area

1. Concentrate enough armed forces to destroy or to expel the main body of armed insurgents.

2. Detach for the area sufficient troops to oppose an insurgent's comeback in strength, install these troops in the hamlets, villages, and towns where the population lives.

3. Establish contact with the population, control its movements in order to cut off its links with the guerrillas.

4. Destroy the local insurgent political organizations.

5. Set up, by means of elections, new provisional local authorities.

6. Test these authorities by assigning them various concrete tasks. Replace the softs and the incompetents, give full support to the active leaders. Organize self-defense units.

7. Group and educate the leaders in a national political movement.

8. Win over or suppress the last insurgent remnants.

Order having been re-established in the area, the process may be repeated elsewhere. It is not necessary, for that matter, to wait until the last point has been completed.

The operations outlined above will be studied in more detail, but let us first discuss this strategy. Like every similar concept, this one may be sound in theory but dangerous when applied rigidly to a specific case. It is difficult, however, to deny its logic because the laws—or shall we say the facts—on which it is based can be easily recognized in everyday political life and in every recent revolutionary war.

This strategy is also designed to cope with the worst case that can confront a counterinsurgent, i.e., suppressing an insurgency in what was called a "red" area, where the insurgent is already in full control of the population. Some of the operations suggested can obviously be skipped in the "pink" areas, most can be skipped in the "white" ones. However, the general order in which they must be conducted cannot be tampered with under normal conditions without violating the principles of counterinsurgency warfare and of plain common sense. For instance, small detachments of troops cannot be installed in villages so long as the insurgent is able to gather a superior force and to overpower a detachment in a surprise attack; Step 2 obviously has to come after Step 1. Nor can elections be staged when the insurgent cells still exist, for the elections would most likely bring forth the insurgent's stooges.

Economy of Forces

Because these operations are spread in time, they can be spread in space. This strategy thus conforms with the principle of economy of forces, a vital one in a war where the insurgent needs so little to achieve so much whereas the counterinsurgent needs so much to achieve so little.

While a main effort is made in the selected area, necessarily at some risk to the other areas, what results can the counterinsurgent legitimately expect from his operations in these other areas? To prevent the insurgent from developing into a higher form of warfare, that is to say, from organizing a regular army. This objective is fulfilled when the insurgent is denied safe bases, and it can be achieved by purely conventional raids that do not tie down large counterinsurgent forces.

Through this strategy, insurgency can be rolled back with increased strength and momentum, for as soon as an area has been made safe, important forces can be withdrawn and transferred to the neighboring areas, swollen with locally recruited loyal and tested personnel. The transfer of troops can begin as soon as the first step is concluded.

Irreversibility

The myth of Sisyphus is a recurrent nightmare for the counterinsurgent. By following the strategy just outlined, the counterinsurgent introduces some measure of irreversibility in his operations. When troops live among the population and give it protection until the population is able to protect itself with a minimum of outside support, the insurgent's power cannot easily be rebuilt, and this in itself is no mean achievement. But the turning point really comes when leaders have emerged from the population and have committed themselves on the side of the counterinsurgent. They can be counted upon because they have proved their loyalty in deeds and not in words, and because they have everything to lose from a return of the insurgents.

Initiative

This is an offensive strategy, and it inevitably aims at regaining the initiative from the insurgent. On the national scale, this is so because the counterinsurgent is free to select the area of main effort; as soon as he does it, he no longer submits himself to the insurgent's will. It is so equally on the local scale because he confronts the insurgent with a dilemma: accepting the challenge, and thus a defensive posture, or leaving the area and being powerless to oppose the counterinsurgent's action on the population.

In conventional warfare, when the Blues attack the Reds on Point A, the Reds can relieve the pressure by attacking the Blues on Point B, and the Blues cannot escape the counterpressure. In revolutionary warfare, when the insurgent exerts pressure in Area A, the counterinsurgent cannot relieve the pressure by attacking the insurgent on Area B. The insurgent simply refuses to accept the fight, and he can refuse because of his fluidity. The Chinese Nationalists' offensive against Yenan in 1947 is an example; when the Vietminh started pressing against Dien Bien Phu in northeastern Indochina, the French command launched Operation Atlante against the Vietminh areas in Central Vietnam; Atlante had no effect on the other battle.

However, when the counterinsurgent applies pressure not on the insurgent directly but on the population, which is the insurgent's real source of strength, the insurgent cannot so freely refuse the fight because he courts defeat.

Full Utilization of the Counterinsurgent's Assets

If the insurgent is fluid, the population is not. By concentrating his efforts on the population, the counterinsurgent minimizes his rigidity and makes full use of his assets. His administrative capabilities, his economic resources, his information and propaganda media, his military superiority due to heavy weapons and large units, all of which are cumbersome and relatively useless against the elusive insurgent, recover their full value when applied to the task of obtaining the support of a static population. What does it matter if the counterinsurgent is unable on the whole to run as fast as the insurgent? What counts is the fact that the insurgent cannot dislodge a better-armed detachment of counterinsurgents from a village, or cannot harass it enough to make the counterinsurgent unable to devote most of his energy to the population.

Simplicity

Why is there so little intellectual confusion in conventional warfare while there has been so much in the past counterinsurgencies? Two explanations may be advanced: When a conventional war starts, the abrupt transition from peace to war and the very nature of the war clarify most of the problems for the contending sides, particularly for the defender. The issue, whatever it was, becomes now a matter of defeating the enemy. The objective, insofar as it is essentially military, is the destruction of his forces and the occupation of his territory; such an objective provides clear-cut criteria to assess gains, stagnation, or losses. The way to reach it is by military action supported by diplomacy and economic blockade. The national organization for war is simple: The government directs, the military executes, the nation provides the tools.

We have seen that this cannot be the case in counterinsurgency warfare. Transition from peace to war is very gradual, the issue is never clear, the objective is the population, military and political actions cannot be separated, and military action—essential though it is—cannot be the main form of action.

Conventional warfare has been thoroughly analyzed in the course of centuries—indeed for almost the entire extent of recorded history—and the process of battle has been sliced into distinct phases: march toward the enemy, contact with the enemy, test of the enemy's strength, attack, exploitation of success, eventually retreat, etc. The student learns in military schools what he has to do in each phase, according to the latest doctrine. Field games are staged to give him practical training in the maneuvers he may have to conduct. When he is in the field under actual war conditions, his intellectual problem amounts to determining which phase of the battle he finds himself in; then he applies to his particular situation the general rules governing the phase. His talent, his judgment come into play only here.

This has not yet been done for counterinsurgency warfare. Who indeed has heard of field games involving the task of winning the support of the population when such a task, which, in any event, requires months of continuous efforts, has no clear built-in criteria to assess the results of the games? And who is going to play the part of the population?

Simplicity in concept and in execution are important requirements for any counterinsurgency doctrine The proposed strategy appears to meet them. For it is not enough to give a broad definition of the goal (to get the support of the population); it is just as necessary to show how to reach it (by finding and organizing the people who are actively in favor of the counterinsurgent), and in such a way as to allow a margin of initiative to the counterinsurgent personnel who implement the strategy—and they are a widely mixed group of politicians, civil servants, economists, social workers, soldiers—yet with enough precision to channel their efforts in a single direction. The division of the over-all action into successive steps following each other in logical order facilitates the tactical tasks of the agents; they know at each step what the intermediate objective is and what they have to do to reach it.

To Command Is to Control

With the step-by-step approach, the counterinsurgent provides himself with a way of assessing at any time the situation and the progress made. He can thus exert his control and conduct the war by switching means from an advanced area to a retarded one, by giving larger responsibilities to the subordinate leaders who have proved successful, and by removing those who have failed. In other words, he can command because he can verify.

What could happen in default of control? The general counterinsurgency effort would produce an *accidental* mosaic, a patchwork of pieces with one well pacified, next to it another one not so pacified or perhaps even under the effective insurgent's control: an ideal situation for the insurgent, who will be able to maneuver at will among the pieces, concentrating on some, temporarily vanishing from others. The *intentional* mosaic created by necessity when the counterinsurgent concentrates his efforts in a selected area is in itself a great enough source of difficulties without adding to it in the selected area.

NOTE

1. Except, of course, the psychological handicap, which can be alleviated only by the protraction of the war. To solve it would require that the counterinsurgent espouse the insurgent's cause without losing his power at the same time. If it were possible to do so, then the insurgent's cause was a bad one to start with, tactically speaking.

Chapter 6

FROM STRATEGY TO TACTICS

COMMAND PROBLEMS

Single Direction

Destroying or expelling from an area the main body of the guerrilla forces, preventing their return, installing garrisons to protect the population, tracking the guerrilla remnants—these are predominantly military operations.

Identifying, arresting, interrogating the insurgent political agents, judging them, rehabilitating those who can be won over—these are police and judicial tasks.

Establishing contact with the population, imposing and enforcing control measures, organizing local elections, testing the new leaders, organizing them into a party, doing all the constructive work needed to win the wholehearted support of the population—these are primarily political operations.

The expected result—final defeat of the insurgents—is not an addition but a multiplication of these various operations; they all are essential and if one is nil, the product will be zero. Clearly, more than any other kind of warfare, counterinsurgency must respect the principle of a single direction. A single boss must direct the operations from beginning until the end.

The problem, unfortunately, is not simple. Tasks and responsibilities cannot be neatly divided between the civilian and the soldier, for their operations overlap too much with each other. The soldier does not stay in his garrison with nothing to do, once the early large-scale operations have been concluded; he constantly patrols, ambushes, combs out; at some time in the process, he will have to organize, equip, train, and lead self-defense units. The policeman starts gathering intelligence right from the beginning; his role does not end when the political cells have been destroyed, because the insurgent will keep trying to build new ones. The civil servant does not wait to start his work until the army has cleared away the guerrillas.

Furthermore, no operation can be strictly military or political, if only because they each have psychological effects that alter the over-all situation for better or for worse. For instance, if the judge prematurely releases unrepentent insurgents, the effects will soon be felt by the policeman, the civil servant, and the soldier.

Another fact complicates the situation. However developed the civil administration may be in peacetime, it is never up to the personnel requirements of a courterinsurgency. When the broad objective of winning the support of the population is translated into concrete field tasks, each multiplied by the given number of villages, towns, and districts, the number of reliable personnel needed is staggering. Usually, the armed forces alone can supply them promptly. As a result, the counterinsurgent government is exposed to a dual temptation: to assign political, police, and other tasks to the armed forces; to let the military direct the entire process—if not in the whole country, at least in some areas.

The first one cannot be avoided. To confine soldiers to purely military functions while urgent and vital tasks have to be done, and nobody else is available to undertake them, would be senseless. The soldier must then be prepared to become a propagandist, a social worker, a civil engineer, a schoolteacher, a nurse, a boy scout. But only for as long as he cannot be replaced, for it is better to entrust civilian tasks to civilians. This, incidentally, is what the Chinese Communists have always tended to do. During the spring and summer of 1949, on the eve of their drive into south China, they recruited and trained in special schools more than 50,000 students whose mission was to follow the army and assist it by taking over "army servicing, publicity work, education and mobilization of the masses."[1] To imitate this example is not easy for the counterinsurgent. Where does one find such a large group of reliable civilians when the loyalty of almost everyone is open to question? But it will have to be done eventually. The second temptation—to let the military direct the entire process—on the other hand, is so dangerous that it must be resisted at all costs.

Primacy of the Political over the Military Power

That the political power is the undisputed boss is a matter of both principle and practicality. What is at stake is the country's political regime, and to defend it is a political affair. Even if this requires military action, the action is constantly directed toward a political goal. Essential though it is, the military action is secondary to the political one, its primary purpose being to afford the political power enough freedom to work safely with the population.

The armed forces are but one of the many instruments of the counterinsurgent, and what is better than the political power to harness the non-military instruments, to see that appropriations come at the right time to consolidate the military work, that political and social reforms follow through?

"A revolutionary war is 20 per cent military action and 80 per cent political" is a formula that reflects the truth. Giving the soldier authority over the civilian would thus contradict one of the major characteristics of this type of war. In practice, it would inevitably tend to reverse the relative importance of military versus political action and move the counterinsurgent's warfare closer to a conventional one. Were the armed forces the instrument of a party and their leaders high-ranking members of the party, controlled and assisted by political commissars having their own direct channel to the party's central direction, then giving complete authority to the military might work; however, this describes the general situation of the insurgent, not of his opponent.

It would also be self-defeating, for it would mean that the counterinsurgent government had acknowledged a signal defeat: Unable to cope with the insurgency through normal government structures, it would have abdicated in favor of the military who, at once, become the prime and easy target of the insurgent propaganda. It would be a miracle if, under these circumstances, the insurgent did not succeed in divorcing the soldier from the nation.

The inescapable conclusion is that the over-all responsibility should stay with the civilian power at every possible level. If there is a shortage of trusted officials, nothing prevents filling the gap with military personnel serving in a civilian capacity. If the worst comes to the worst, the fiction, at least, should be preserved.

Coordination of Efforts

The counterinsurgent leader, whom we now assume to be a civilian, has to take into account the problems of the various civilian and military components of his forces before reaching a decision, especially when their actions interrelate intricately and when their demands often conflict with each other. He has also to coordinate and to channel their efforts in a single direction. How can he do it? Among the theoretical solutions in terms of organization, two are obvious: (1) the committee, as in Malaya, for example, where control of an area at district level was invested in a committee under the chairmanship of the district officer, with the members drawn from the police, local civilians (European planters and representative Chinese and Malayans), and the soldiers; (2) or the integrated civilian-military staff, where the soldier is directly subordinated to the local civil authority (the author knows of no example of this setup, but the opposite case—with the civil authority directly subordinated to the local military one—is easy to find, as in the Philippines, where army officers took the place of a nonexistent civil administration, or in Algeria, where all powers were invested in the military for a brief period in 1958–59).

Each formula has its merits and its defects. A committee[2] is flexible, affords more freedom to its members, and can be kept small, but it is slow. An integrated staff allows a more direct line of command and is speedier, but it is more rigid and prone to bureaucratism. There seems to be room for both in counterinsurgency warfare. The committee is better for the higher echelons concerned with long- and medium-range affairs, the integrated staff for the lower echelons, where speed is essential. For counterinsurgency, at the bottom levels, is a very small-scale war, with small-scale and fugitive opportunities that must be seized upon instantly.

At the higher echelons, where the committee system prevails and where the civilian and military components retain their separate structures, they should each be organized in such a way as to promote their cooperation still more. In conventional warfare, the staff of a large military unit is composed roughly of two main branches—"intelligence/operations" and "logistics." In counterinsurgency warfare, there is a desperate need for a third branch—the "political" one—which would have the same weight as the others. The officer in charge of it would follow the developments in all matters pertaining to political and civic action, advise his chief, make his voice heard when operations are in the planning stage and not have to wait until they are too advanced to be altered. Similarly, the civilian staff, which in conventional warfare usually has little to do with military affairs, should have its military branch, with a corresponding role toward the civilian chief. With these two organic branches working closely together, the danger of divergent efforts by the civilian and the military might be reduced.

Whatever system is chosen, however, the best organization is only as good as its members. Even with the best conceivable organization, personality conflicts are more than likely to be the order of the day. Although the wrong member can sometimes be fired and replaced, this will not solve the problem for all committees or integrated staff.

The question, then, is how to make these mixed organizations work at their maximum effectiveness in a counterinsurgency, regardless of the personality factors. Assuming that each of these organizations works more or less with its own over-all personality, how is the disjointed, mosaic effect of their operations to be avoided? If the individual members of the organizations were of the same mind, if every organization worked according to a standard pattern, the problem would be solved. Is this not precisely what a coherent, well-understood, and accepted doctrine would tend to achieve? More than anything else, a doctrine appears to be the practical answer to the problem of how to channel efforts in a single direction.

Primacy of the Territorial Command

The counterinsurgent's armed forces have to fulfill two different missions: to break the military power of the insurgent and to ensure the safety of the territory in each area. It seems natural that the counterinsurgent's forces should be organized into two types of units, the mobile ones fighting in a rather conventional fashion, and the static ones staying with the population in order to protect it and to supplement the political efforts.

The static units are obviously those that know best the local situation, the population, the local problems; if a mistake is made, they are the ones who will bear the consequences. It follows that when a mobile unit is sent to operate temporarily in an area, it must come under the territorial command, even if the military commander of the area is the junior officer. In the same way as the U.S. ambassador is the boss of every U.S. organization operating in the country to which he is accredited, the territorial military commander must be the boss of all military forces operating in his area.

Adaptation of the Armed Forces to
Counterinsurgency Warfare

As long as the insurgent has failed to build a powerful regular army, the counterinsurgent has little use for heavy, sophisticated forces designed for conventional warfare. For his ground forces, he needs infantry and more infantry, highly mobile and lightly armed; some field artillery for occasional support; armored cavalry, and if terrain conditions are favorable, horse cavalry for road surveillance and patrolling. For his air force, he wants ground support and observation planes of slow speed, high endurance, great firepower, protected against small-arms ground fire; plus short-takeoff transport planes and helicopters, which play a vital role in counterinsurgency operations. The navy's mission, if any, is to enforce a blockade, a conventional type of operation that does not require elaboration here. In addition, the counterinsurgent needs an extremely dense signal network.

The counterinsurgent, therefore, has to proceed to a first transformation of his existing forces along these lines, notably to convert into infantry units as many unneeded specialized units as possible.

The adaptation, however, must go deeper than that. At some point in the counterinsurgency process, the static units that took part initially in large-scale military operations in their area will find themselves confronted with a huge variety of nonmilitary tasks which have to be performed in order to get the support of the population, and which can be performed only by military personnel, because of the shortage of reliable civilian political and administrative personnel. Making a thorough census, enforcing new regulations on movements of persons and goods, informing the population, conducting person-to-person propaganda, gathering intelligence on the insurgent's political agents, implementing the various economic and social reforms, etc.—all these will become their primary activity. They have to be organized, equipped, and supported accordingly. Thus, a mimeograph machine may turn out to be more useful than a machine gun, a soldier trained as a pediatrician more important than a mortar expert, cement more wanted than barbed wire, clerks more in demand than riflemen.

Adaptation of Minds

If the forces have to be adapted to their new missions, it is just as important that the minds of the leaders and men—and this includes the civilian as well as the military—be adapted also to the special demands of counterinsurgency warfare.

Reflexes and decisions that would be considered appropriate for the soldier in conventional warfare and for the civil servant in normal times are not necessarily the right ones in counterinsurgency situations. A soldier fired upon in conventional war who does not fire back with every available weapon would be guilty of a dereliction of his duty; the reverse would be the case in counterinsurgency warfare, where the rule is to apply the minimum of fire. "No politics" is an ingrained reaction for the conventional soldier, whose job is solely to defeat the enemy; yet in counterinsurgency warfare, the soldier's job is to help win the support of the population, and in so doing, he has to engage in practical politics. A system of military awards and promotion, such as that in conventional warfare, which would encourage soldiers to kill or capture the largest number of enemies, and thus induce him to increase the scope and the frequency of his military operations, may well be disastrous in counterinsurgency warfare.

The administrator in peacetime has to preserve a politically neutral attitude toward the population, has to let "a hundred flowers blossom, a hundred schools of thought contend," but not in counterinsurgency, where his duty is to see that only the right flower blossoms and not the weed, at least until the situation becomes normal again.

The counterinsurgent government clearly needs leaders who understand the nature of the war. There are two possible ways to get them: by indoctrination and training in the technique of counterinsurgency warfare, and by a priori or natural selection.

The theory of counterinsurgency warfare can be taught like that of any other type of war, and of course, the counterinsurgent must see that it is taught to the entire personnel of his military and civilian forces. The difficulty arises in connection with giving practical training to the students. It is easy to stage exercises and games related to the military operations required in counterinsurgency warfare, but it is hardly possible to duplicate in a realistic way the setting for the nonmilitary operations. For one thing, the population with its behavior and its mood is the major factor in these operations. How can this be introduced in the game? Also, decisions taken in the nonmilitary operations seldom produce immediate effects, whereas the soundness of a military decision in the field can be assessed almost immediately. Most of the training will have to be done on the job. More will be said on this question in the next chapter.

Indoctrination and training, however, are slow processes, and the need for able leaders is immediate. There are no easy criteria enabling one to determine in advance whether a man who has not been previously involved in a counterinsurgency will be a good leader. A workable solution is to identify those who readily accept the new concepts of counterinsurgency warfare and give them responsibility. Those who then prove themselves in action should be pushed upward.

There is room in the armed forces, but not in the civilian component of the counterinsurgent force, for the cadres who cannot shed their conventional-warfare thinking. They can be assigned to the mobile units.

Needless to say, if political reliability is a problem, as it may well be in a revolutionary war, it is the most reliable cadres who should be assigned to work with the population.

SELECTION OF THE AREA OF EFFORTS

The Strategic Problem

Two opposite approaches are open to the counterinsurgent, and a third which is a compromise between the others. According to the first approach, one proceeds from the difficult to the easy. Efforts are concentrated initially in the red areas and progressively extended to the pink and white ones. It is the fastest way, if it succeeds. The other approach, from the easy to the difficult, requires fewer means at the outset, but it is slower and gives more opportunity for the insurgent to develop and to consolidate in the red areas. The choice between the approaches depends essentially on the relative strength of the opponents.

During the Greek War, the Nationalists chose initially a compromise heavily accented toward the first approach. They started by tackling the region of Thessaly in central Greece; immediately after that, they moved east and north against the Communist strongholds established along the borders. The Communists withdrew safely into satellites' territories and reappeared elsewhere. The first Nationalist offensive failed. In their second attempt in 1949–50, the Nationalists adopted the opposite strategy: They eliminated the Communists from the Peloponnesus, then operated in greater strength in Thessaly, and finally cleaned the border regions. This time they succeeded, thanks in part to the defection of Tito from the Soviet bloc, which prevented the Greek Communists from playing hide and seek on his territory.

When the revolutionary war resumed in China after the Japanese surrender, the Nationalists had the choice between three courses of action:

1. Concentrating their efforts in Manchuria, the area most remote from the Nationalists' center of power, and where the Communist forces, armed with Japanese equipment, were the strongest.
2. Cleaning up central China, then north China, and finally Manchuria.
3. Operating everywhere.

Wide in theory, the choice was narrow in fact, because the Nationalists could not afford to let their opponents develop safely in Manchuria, the richest industrial part of China, where the Communists were in direct contact with the Soviet Union. And as Manchuria had been occupied by Soviet troops in the last days of World War II, the Nationalist Government had to reassert its sovereignty over it. The Nationalists felt compelled to invest their best units in Manchuria.

Whether the Nationalists would have won had they acted otherwise is rather doubtful, for the Chinese Communists were a formidable opponent by 1945. But their chances might have been better if they had adopted the second course of action.

In Algeria, where the French, as of 1956, enjoyed an overwhelming military superiority over the FLN, their efforts were spread initially all over the territory, with larger concentrations along the borders with Tunisia and Morocco and in Kabylia, a rugged, heavily populated mountain area. The FLN forces were soon broken up, but lack of doctrine and experience in what to do after military operations, among other things, precluded a clear-cut French success. In 1959–60, the French strategy proceeded from West to East, starting with the Oran region, then to the Ouarsenis Mountains, to Kabylia, and finally, to the Constantine region. This time, there was enough experience; the period of muddling through was over. By the end of 1960, when the French Government policy had switched from "defeating the insurgency" to "disengaging France from Algeria," the FLN forces in Algeria were reduced to between 8,000 and 9,000 men well isolated from the population, broken into tiny, ineffective bands, with 6,500 weapons, most of which had been buried for lack of ammunition; not a single *wilaya* (region) boss in Algeria was in contact with the FLN organization abroad, not even by radio; purges were devastating their ranks, and some of the high-ranking FLN chiefs in Algeria made overtures to surrender. The borders were closed to infiltration, except very occasionally by one or two men. The French forces included 150,000 Moslems, not counting self-defense groups in almost every village. All that would have remained to do, if the policy had not changed, was to eliminate the diehard insurgent remnants, a long task at best, considering the size of Algeria and its terrain. In Malaya, this final phase of the counterinsurgency lasted at least five years.

The selection of the first area of efforts must obviously be influenced first of all by the strategic approach chosen. It is well to remember, in any case, that the counterinsurgent needs a clear-cut, even if geographically limited, success as soon as possible. In terms of psychological benefit to the course of the revolutionary war, it is worth taking this risk even if it means letting the insurgent develop in some other area.

The counterinsurgent, who usually has no practical experience in the nonmilitary operations required in counterinsurgency warfare, must acquire it fast.

These two considerations indicate that the choice of the first area should promise an easy tactical victory at the price of a strategic risk. In other words, it seems better to go from the easy to the difficult unless the counterinsurgent is so strong that he can afford the opposite strategy.

The Tactical Factors

In selecting the area, factors customarily taken into account in conventional warfare, such as terrain, transportation facilities, climate, remain valid. In this respect, the counterinsurgent must pay particular attention to whether the area can be easily isolated and compartmented by taking advantage of natural obstacles, sea, rivers, plains. It may seem strange that plains should be considered as natural obstacles in war, but the fact is that mountains, forests, and swamps are not obstacles for the insurgent, but rather his favorite ground. Nor are international boundaries barriers; usually, these have restricted only the counterinsurgent. If natural obstacles are lacking, consideration must be given to building artificial ones, as the French did along the Tunisian and Moroccan borders. This solution may be expensive, but it results in so much security and such a saving in manpower that it may be worth it.

However, since the population is the objective, factors pertaining to it acquire a particular importance. There are objective factors. How large is the population? The larger it is, the higher the stakes. Is the population concentrated in towns and villages, or dispersed all over the terrain? A concentrated population is easier to protect and control; thus an infantry company can easily control a small town of 10,000–20,000 inhabitants—short of a general uprising—but it would take a much larger unit if the same population were spread over the countryside. How dependent is the population on outside supplies and on economic facilities provided by the counterinsurgent administration? Does it have to import food and other material? Is trade important, or can it live in an autarchic economy?

Above all, there are subjective factors. How does the population view the respective opponents? What are the proportions of potential friends, neutrals, enemies? Can these categories be defined in advance? Can it, for instance, be assumed that the bourgeoisie, the rich farmers, the small farmers, etc., will take this attitude or that? Is there any leverage over them? Are there any divisive factors by which any of these categories can further be dissociated by either of the opponents? This sort of political analysis is as important in counterinsurgency walfare as map study is in conventional warfare, for it will determine, however roughly, whether the area considered will be easy or difficult to work on. In Algeria, for instance, it was automatically assumed that Moslem veterans who received a pension from the French Government would be hostile to the FLN, that Moslem women living in slavery under Islamic customs would welcome their emancipation. In spite of partial setbacks, these assumptions proved generally true.

There is an optimum dimension for the size of both the area and the population. Above it, isolation would be difficult to maintain and the efforts would be too diluted. Below it, insurgent influence would keep penetrating too easily from the outside, and the population, conscious of its small number and feeling too exposed and too conspicuous, would be reluctant to lean on the counterinsurgent side.

The right size cannot be determined in the abstract; it varies too much from case to case. The fact that the insurgent usually moves on foot provides, however, a rough yardstick. The minimum diameter of the area should be equal to no less than three days' march so that outside guerrillas trying to infiltrate deeply would be forced to march more than one night. This would give the counterinsurgent more chance to catch them.

POLITICAL PREPARATION

On the eve of embarking on a major effort, the counterinsurgent faces what is probably the most difficult problem of the war: He has to arm himself with a competing cause.

Let us first eliminate the easy cases—easy as analytical problems— briefly described as follows:

1. The insurgent has really no cause at all; he is exploiting the counterinsurgent's weaknesses and mistakes. Such seems to be the situation in South Vietnam today. The Vietcong cannot clamor for land, which is plentiful in South Vietnam; nor raise the banner of anticolonialism, for South Vietnam is no longer a colony; nor offer Communism, which does not appear to be very popular with the North Vietnamese population. The insurgent's program is simply: "Throw the rascals out." If the "rascals" (whoever is in power in Saigon) amend their ways, the insurgent would lose his cause.

2. The insurgent has a cause that the counterinsurgent can espouse without unduly endangering his power. This was, as we have seen, the situation in the Philippines during the Huks' insurgency. All the counterinsurgent has to do is to promise the necessary reforms and prove that he means it.

We are left with the general case when the insurgent has the monopoly of a dynamic cause. What can the counterinsurgent do? Knowing that his ideological handicap will somewhat subside as the war itself becomes the main issue is no consolation because he has to last until then, and the time to launch a counteroffensive is at the start.

It would be a mistake to believe that a counterinsurgent cannot get the population's support unless he concedes political reforms. However unpopular he may be, if he is sufficiently strong-willed and powerful, if he can rely on a small but active core of supporters who remain loyal to him because they would lose everything including their lives if the insurgent wins, he can maintain himself in power. He may very well withdraw whatever benefits the population receives from the mere existence of his regime—a measure of law and order, a more-or-less running economy, functioning public works and services, etc.—and restore them gradually as a premium for the population's cooperation. He may, for instance, ration food and see that only those who cooperate receive ration cards. He may, at the same time, utilize to the utmost those who are willing to support him actively, giving them increased privileges and power, and ruling through them, however disliked they may be. This is the way the Kadar regime in Hungary and others, no doubt, keep themselves in power. But such a policy of pure force could bring at best a precarious return to the *status quo ante,* a state of perpetual tension, not a lasting peace.

In default of liberal inclinations and of a sense of justice—if there is some justice in the insurgent's demands—wisdom and expediency demand that the counterinsurgent equip himself with a political program designed to take as much wind as possible out of the insurgent's sails. This raises serious questions of substance and timing.

When looking for a countercause, the counterinsurgent is left with a narrow choice of secondary issues that appeal almost invariably to reason at a time when passion is the prime mover. And how far can he go in the way of reforms without endangering his power, which, after all, is what he—right or wrong—is fighting to retain? When the insurgent's cause is an all-or-nothing proposition, as in most anticolonial or Communist-led insurgencies, the margin for political maneuver is extremely limited. The insurgent wants independence today, speaks of revolution, promotes class struggle and the dictatorship of the proletariat; his opponent can offer only internal autonomy or some variation of it, insist on evolution, stress fraternity of all classes.

Yet, knowing that his program will have no or little immediate appeal, the counterinsurgent must somehow find a set of reforms, even if secondary, even if minor. He has to gamble that reason, in the long run, will prevail over passion.

He would be wise also to ascertain whether what he offers is really wanted by the people. Reforms conceived in the abstract at a high level may often sound promising on paper but do not always correspond to the popular wish. A practical method, therefore, would consist in investigating objectively the people's demands, making a list of them, crossing out those that cannot be granted safely and promoting the rest.

The counterinsurgent must also decide when to publicize his program. If he does this too early, it could be taken for a sign of weakness, raise the insurgent's demands, even encourage the population into supporting the insurgent in the hope of more concessions; and as the war lasts, the impact of the program would blur. If the announcement is unduly delayed, the task of winning the support of the population would become more difficult. Appreciating the right time is a matter of judgment based on circumstances, and no solution can be suggested in advance. It seems possible and judicious, however, to separate the political program from the specific concrete reforms. The program could be announced early in general terms. The reforms, since they are meaningless unless they can safely be implemented, could be publicized locally as soon as the preliminary military operations have been concluded; they should be publicized nationally when local experience has shown their value.

In any case, nothing could be worse than promising reforms and being unwilling or unable to implement them.

THE FIRST AREA AS A TEST AREA

However prepared, trained, and indoctrinated the counterinsurgent forces may be, reality will always differ from theory. Mistakes are bound to happen, but it would be inexcusable not to learn from them. This is why the first area selected must be considered a test area. The value of the operations conducted there lies just as much in what they teach as in their intrinsic results.

Testing means experimenting, being intent on watching objectively what takes place, being prompt and willing to alter what goes wrong. And learning implies drawing the proper lessons from the events and spreading the experience among others. All this cannot be left to chance and personal initiative; it must be organized carefully and deliberately.

The Chinese Communists, who used to be well aware of the importance of learning and combining theory with practice, seem to have applied in the early 1950's a method that owes little to Marxism and much to experimental science and plain common sense. They never explicitly explained their method, so what follows is a reconstruction based on observation of facts and on some logical guessing.

Whenever the top Chinese Communist leadership, i.e., the ten or twelve members of the standing group of the Central Committee, considered a major reform—for instance, the establishment of semisocialist agricultural cooperatives—the idea was first discussed thoroughly within the group. If it was not rejected there, a preliminary draft, Project No. 1, would be submitted next to the Central Committee with its seventy or so regular members, again thoroughly discussed, amended, or perhaps even discarded.

Out of the discussion would come a Project No. 2, which would be submitted then to a vertical slice of the Party composed of members selected from every level and every area of China. In typical Chinese Communist fashion, open and sincere discussion would be compulsory; one could not just approve without giving personal and convincing reasons. Such a broadening of viewpoints would, of course, produce further modifications of the project, or again reveal its impracticality. Out of this would come Project No. 3.

The Chinese Communists had early designated certain areas of every size as test areas. Thus, Manchuria as a whole was a test region because it was considered the vanguard for the industrialization of China; a province here and there, one or several districts in each province, one or several villages in each district had been selected for various reasons: because they were ideologically advanced, or average, or backward; because they were close to a large city or were populated by ethnic minorities. Project No. 3 would be implemented secretly in the test areas, with a minimum of local publicity. The operations would be watched by cadres of every level coming from the nontest areas.

At the end of the experiment, a thorough critique would be made and the project rejected altogether or modified according to the lessons of the experiment. If kept, it would be now announced as an official decision and applied with fanfare all over the country. The observers would return to their posts, not to carry out the reform by themselves but to serve as teachers and inspectors at their respective levels for the mass of local cadres.

This is how Peking was able to conduct in a few weeks the first relatively thorough census of China,[3] or impose within a month a tight rationing of grain. The fact that the Communist regime literally ran amuck in the subsequent period of the "Great Leap Forward" does not destroy the validity of the principle. And although the above example is not drawn from a counterinsurgency situation, the principle could indeed be used with profit in any counterinsurgency.

NOTES

1. General Chang Ting-chen, chief of the South China Service Corps, member of the Central Committee, as quoted in *The New York Times,* July 4, 1949.

2. After the above stress on the necessity for a boss at every level in counterinsurgency warfare, a committee must be seen in this case not as an organization where decisions are reached by vote, but merely as a convenient place to air problems for the benefit of the boss.

3. If the thoroughness of the census cannot be doubted, the veracity of the published results is another affair. Only the Red Chinese know the exact truth.

Chapter 7

THE OPERATIONS

We shall study here the tactical problems normally arising with the implementation of the strategy outlined in Chapter 4. Dealing with, and in, the abstract, we shall, of course, be more concerned with principles than with actual recipes.

THE FIRST STEP: DESTRUCTION OR EXPULSION OF THE INSURGENT FORCES

The destruction of the guerrilla forces in the selected area is, obviously, highly desirable, and this is what the counterinsurgent must strive for. One thing should be clear, however: This operation is not an end in itself, for guerrillas, like the heads of the legendary hydra, have the special ability to grow again if not all destroyed at the same time. The real purpose of the first operation, then, is to prepare the stage for the further development of the counterinsurgent action.

The goal is reached when static units left to garrison the area can safely deploy to the extent necessary. Consequently, if most of the guerrillas are merely expelled, the result is still good. If they disband into very small groups and stay hidden in the area, the situation is still acceptable as long as the counterinsurgent sees to it that they cannot regroup. To this effect, in this case, some of the counterinsurgent mobile forces will have to remain in the area until the static units, having become well established and having imposed enough physical control over the population, are in a position to cope with the dispersed guerrillas and to prevent their regrouping into larger, more dangerous gangs.

The first step in the counterinsurgent's operations should not be allowed to drag on for the sake of achieving better military results.

Tactics for this operation are simple in essence.

1. Mobile units, plus units earmarked to stay in the area in order to reinforce whatever static units were originally there, are suddenly concentrated around the area. They start operating from the outside in, aiming at catching the guerrillas in a ring. At the same time, units garrisoning the adjoining areas are ordered to intensify their activity on the periphery of the selected area.

2. The sweep is next conducted from the inside out, aiming at least at expelling the guerrillas.

3. The over-all operation is finally broken down into several small-scale ones. All the static units, the original as well as the new ones, are assigned to their permanent sectors. A part of the mobile units operates as a body, centrally controlled; the rest is lent to the sectors. All the forces work on what is left of the guerrillas after the two earlier sweeps.

The operations are supplemented during this step—as in all the others—by tactical information and psychological warfare directed at the insurgent, the counterinsurgent's own forces, and the population.

Propaganda Directed at the Counterinsurgent Forces

The operations during this step, being predominantly of a military nature, will inevitably cause some damage and destruction. The insurgent on his part will strive to provoke clashes between the population and the counterinsurgent forces.

Since antagonizing the population will not help, it is imperative that hardships for it and rash actions on the part of the forces be kept to a minimum. The units participating in the operations should be thoroughly indoctrinated to that effect, the misdeeds punished severely and even publicly if this can serve to impress the population. Any damage done should be immediately compensated without red tape.

Propaganda Directed at the Population

To ask the local people to cooperate en masse and openly at this stage would be useless and even self-defeating, for they cannot do it, being still under the insurgent's control. Promoting such a line would expose the counterinsurgent to a public failure. Furthermore, if some local civilians were to cooperate prematurely and be punished for it by the insurgent, the psychological setback would be disastrous.

The counterinsurgent would be wiser to limit his goal to obtaining the neutrality of the population, i.e., its passivity toward both sides. The general line could be: "Stay neutral and peace will soon return to the area. Help the insurgent, and we will be obliged to carry on more military operations and thus inflict more destruction."

Propaganda Directed at the Insurgent

The insurgent's worst mistake at this stage would be to accept the fight, to remain active while the counterinsurgent is very strong. The goal of psychological warfare is to prod him into it.

Once the counterinsurgent has lost the benefit of surprise—if any— achieved during the concentration and after the first operations, if he then proclaims his intention to remain in the area in order to work with the population and to win its support, the insurgent, fearing the loss of face as well as the eventual loss of genuine strength, may be incited to accept the challenge.

THE SECOND STEP: DEPLOYMENT OF THE STATIC UNIT

Complete elimination of the guerrillas by military action being practically impossible at this stage, remnants will always manage to stay in the area, and new recruits will join their ranks so long as the political cells have not been destroyed. They can be conclusively wiped out only with the active cooperation of the population, cooperation which will be available to the counterinsurgent in the later steps of the process, if all goes well. This is why the counterinsurgent forces must now switch their attention from the guerrillas to the population.

This does not mean that military activity will stop. On the contrary, the static units will continue tracking the guerrillas, but now through small-scale operations and ambushes, with the understanding that this activity must never distract them from their primary mission, which is to win the support of the population.

The counterinsurgent also has to see that guerrilla forces do not come back in strength from the outside. Opposing such incursions will be the main task of the area's own mobile forces.

The purpose in deploying static units is to establish a grid of troops so that the population and the counterinsurgent political teams are reasonably well protected, and so that the troops can participate in civic action at the lowest level, just where civilian political personnel is insufficient in number. The area will be divided into sectors and subsectors, each with its own static unit.

The subdivision should be carried out down to the level of the "basic unit of counterinsurgency warfare": the largest unit whose leader is in direct and continuous contact with the population. This is the most important unit in counterinsurgency operations, the level where most of the practical problems arise, where the war is won or lost. The size varies from case to case, and in each case with the situation; the basic unit may be a battalion or a company initially, a squad or even a rural policeman at the end of the process.

Certain points require particular attention in the deployment of static units.

The administrative and the military limits should coincide at every level even if the resulting borders seem nonsensical from a strictly military point of view. Failure to observe this principle would result in confusion that would benefit the insurgent.

It seems logical that the grid be initially tighter in the center of the area than at the periphery, where the counterinsurgent forces will necessarily devote a greater part of their activity to military operations.

The units must be deployed where the population actually lives and not on positions deemed to possess a military value. A military unit can spend the entire war in so-called strategic positions without contributing anything to the insurgent's defeat. This does not mean that bridges, communication centers, and other vulnerable installations should not be protected, of course, but rather that counterinsurgent forces should not be wasted in traditionally commanding positions, for in revolutionary warfare, these positions generally command nothing.

If the rural population is too dispersed to allow the stationing of a military detachment with every group, the counterinsurgent faces the decision of resettling it, as was done in Malaya, Cambodia, and Algeria, and is being done today in South Vietnam. Such a radical measure is complicated and dangerous. Complicated because the population has to be moved, housed, and given facilities to retain its old, or to find new, independent means of living. Dangerous because nobody likes to be uprooted and the operation is bound to antagonize the population seriously at a critical time; a well-planned and well-conducted resettlement may ultimately offer the population economic and social advantages, but they will not become apparent immediately. Moreover, regrouping the population is basically a defensive-minded action. It gives the insurgent a large measure of freedom of the countryside, at least at night, and it is hardly compatible with the ultimate goal of actively using the population, both as a source of intelligence and as a widespread militia, against the guerrillas. A curious illustration of the effects of resettling the population is provided by the Algerian War. When the French sealed off the Tunisian border, they actually built the fence at some distance from it. By removing the local population in some sectors between the fence and the border, they created a no man's land. In 1959, when the situation had improved greatly, they resettled the population in its original dwellings between the fence and the border. Then the FLN, in turn, forcibly removed the population to Tunisia because the French were getting too much intelligence on FLN movements from it.

Resettlement clearly is a last-resort measure, born out of the counterinsurgent's weakness. It should be undertaken only if the trend of the war definitely shows no prospect for the counterinsurgent forces to deploy safely to the required level. If such is the case, resettlement must first be carefully tested in a limited way in order to detect the problems arising with the operation and to get the necessary experience. It should be preceded by intensive psychological and logistical preparation. Finally, the sizes of the various resettlements should correspond to the maximum possible deployment of the counterinsurgent forces; if, for instance, in a given area, a battalion can safely deploy its companies, 4 settlements of 2,000 persons each seem preferable to a single settlement of 8,000.

Areas very sparsely populated and difficult of access because of terrain may be turned into forbidden zones where trespassers can be arrested or eventually shot on sight by ground or air fire.

At every level, the territorial command must have its own mobile reserves. The more dispersed the static units, the more important the mobile reserves are. However, they should not be allowed to remain idle between military operations; they can and should also participate in the civic-action program. In other words, these local mobile reserves are static units on which the local command has an operational option with a specified warning time of one, two, or more hours.

The deployment must not follow a set pattern, such as a company or a platoon for every village. It must be flexible because, as the counterinsurgent work progresses and security increases in the area, the static units will have to spread out more and more, until only a few men will be left to provide the core for self-defense units. Consequently, heavy, expensive constructions for housing the troops should be prohibited, not so much for the cost involved but for psychological reasons. It is only human that soldiers would become attached to their barracks and thus be reluctant to move to less comfortable billets. It is also human that soldiers living in barracks would always appear to the population as outsiders, as people apart. If no construction other than what is strictly necessary is allowed, the counterinsurgent forces will be forced to live like the population, in shacks if necessary, and this will help to create common bonds.

The principle of the test area applies at every level. Until some practical experience has been acquired, it would be best for the basic unit not to spread at once all over its territory, even if it is safe to do so, but instead to concentrate its work first on one village so that the soldiers, when they occupy other villages, will know what to do and what to avoid.

During this step, the following objectives may be assigned to the information and psychological-warfare program.

Propaganda Directed at the Counterinsurgent Forces

As their main efforts will switch hereafter from military to other activities, the counterinsurgent forces need to be told the reasons for the change and to have their future tasks explained to them in general terms. This information program, if conducted in an atmosphere of free discussion, should and could be used for a practical purpose: According to the reactions of the participants, the leader can spot the officers and men who seem best fitted to work closely with the population and those who, on the contrary, are more attracted to the military side of the counterinsurgent work.

Propaganda Directed at the Population

The deployment of static units marks the beginning of a long campaign to shake the population from its neutral, if not hostile, stand. The deployment is a convincing argument to show that the counterinsurgents are there to stay, for they would not spread out if they contemplated leaving the area after an extensive but one-shot operation. This should naturally be the line to exploit, and perhaps the best way might be the indirect one, by letting the population make its own deductions from facts and rumors. For instance, negotiating a two- or three-year contract for billets or land with a villager would surely produce the right effect.

Propaganda Directed at the Insurgent

The deployment cannot be instantaneous or even simultaneous in all the selected area because the situation will inevitably show differences from sector to sector. During this period, the counterinsurgent's concentration of forces is still heavy due to the presence of mobile units operating in the area and to the fact that static units are not yet dispersed into small detachments.

It is still in the counterinsurgent's interest to pursue the same policy as in the preceding step and to incite the guerrillas to react at the worst possible time for them. The point should be stressed, therefore, that they will be lost once they have been cut off from the population. Calling on them to leave the area or to surrender may induce their leaders to do the very opposite, i.e., to fight.

THE THIRD STEP: CONTACT WITH AND CONTROL OF THE POPULATION

Three main objectives are pursued in this step:

1. To re-establish the counterinsurgent's authority over the population.
2. To isolate the population as much as possible, by physical means, from the guerrillas.
3. To gather the necessary intelligence leading to the next step—elimination of the insurgent political cells.

This is the most critical step in the process because of its transitional character, moving from emphasis on military operations to emphasis on political ones, and because it combines a heavy burden of both.

The main center of interest switches now to the level of the basic unit of work, where the real battle takes place.

1. *Contact with the population.* This particular operation, contact with the population, is actually the first confrontation between the two camps for power over the population. The future attitude of the population, hence the probable outcome of the war, is at stake. The counterinsurgent cannot afford to lose this battle.

The battle happens because the population, which was until recently under the insurgent's open control and probably still is under his hidden control through the existing political cells, cannot cooperate spontaneously even if there is every reason to believe that a majority is sympathetic to the counterinsurgent. The inhabitants will usually avoid any contact with him. There is a barrier between them and the counterinsurgent that has to be broken and can be broken only by force. Whatever the counterinsurgent wants the population to do will have to be imposed. Yet the population must not be treated as an enemy.

The solution is first to request, and next to order, the population to perform a certain number of collective and individual tasks that will be paid for. By giving orders, the counterinsurgent provides the alibi that the population needs vis-à-vis the insurgent. A terrible error would be, of course, to issue orders and be unable to enforce them; the counterinsurgent must be careful to issue orders sparingly and only after making sure that the population can humanly comply with them.

Starting with tasks directly benefiting the population—such as cleaning the village or repairing the streets—the counterinsurgent leads the inhabitants gradually, if only in a passive way, to participate in the fight against the insurgent by such work as building roads of military interest, helping in the construction of the village's defensive installations, carrying supplies to military detachments, providing guides and sentries.

2. *Control of the population.* Control of the population begins obviously with a thorough census. Every inhabitant must be registered and given a foolproof identity card. Family booklets should be issued to each household in order to facilitate house-to-house control, and family heads made responsible for reporting any change as it occurs. This last measure is useful not only because it is essential to keep the census up to date, but also because the responsibility placed on the family head makes him participate willy-nilly in the struggle.

The insurgent cannot ignore the census and can guess only too well its implications. He will surely attempt to sabotage it. One way is to force villagers to destroy their new identity cards; since a civilian *sans* identity card is in for much trouble in a revolutionary war, this tactic will soon raise such an outcry among the population that the insurgent will be forced to discard it. He may instead try to register his own personnel, counting on the ignorance of the local counterinsurgent and on the solidarity or silence of the population. To oppose this more insidious tactic, the counterinsurgent can request that every able-bodied man subject to the census be vouched for by two guarantors from outside his family who would be responsible under severe penalty for the veracity of his statements, which should be checked anyway before the identity card is issued. This measure also will contribute to turn the population against the insurgent.

A census, if properly made and exploited, is a basic source of intelligence. It would show, for instance, who is related to whom, an important piece of information in counterinsurgency warfare because insurgent recruiting at the village level is generally based initially on family ties; or who owns property or who works outside of the village and has, therefore, legitimate reasons to travel; or what is each man's source and amount of income, which would immediately separate those who can afford to indulge in abnormal activities from those who cannot. The census should, consequently, be well planned, and conducted in a systematic fashion so that the format and the results do not vary from sector to sector.

The aim of the control is to cut off, or at least reduce significantly, the contacts between the population and the guerrillas. This is done by watching the population's activities; after a while, when the counterinsurgent personnel has become acquainted with the population and knows each inhabitant, unusual behavior can be spotted easily. The process of getting acquainted with the population may be speeded up if the occupied villages are divided into sections, and each assigned to a group of soldiers who will always work there.

Control is also achieved by enforcing a curfew and two simple rules concerning movements of persons: Nobody may leave his village for more than twenty-four hours without a pass, and nobody may receive a stranger from outside the village without permission. The purpose is not to prevent movement—unless there are specific reasons for doing so—but to check on it. By making unchecked travel more difficult, the counterinsurgent again provides the population with a necessary alibi for not helping the insurgent.

These rules, however, have no value unless they can be strictly and systematically enforced. As they are bound to create offenders, a fast and summary system of fines has to be devised and announced to the population. The problem of fines is one that merits consideration at the highest level of the counterinsurgent hierarchy because it is a serious one, and because its solution cannot be left to the initiative of local leaders, for it would lead to too light or too heavy punishment and, in any case, to chaos.

The guerrillas who remain in the selected area at the end of the first step will be few and scattered. They need very little in the way of supplies in order to survive. Cutting them off from their sources would require great effort to produce little result. If control of goods appears necessary, it should be restricted to items that are both scarce and very useful to the guerrillas, such as canned food, radio batteries, shoes. One case when food control is effective at little cost is when the guerrillas are geographically isolated from the population, as in Malaya, where they lived in the jungle while the population had been resettled outside.

3. *Protection of the population.* Just as the counterinsurgent, by forcibly imposing his will on the population, gives it an excuse for not cooperating with the insurgent, the opposite is true. By threatening the population, the insurgent gives the population an excuse, if not a reason, to refuse or refrain from cooperating with the counterinsurgent.

The counterinsurgent cannot achieve much if the population is not, and does not feel, protected against the insurgent. The counterinsurgent needs, therefore, to step up his military activity, to multiply patrols and small-scale operations by day and ambushes by night. Above all, he must avoid the classic situation where he rules during the day and his opponent during the night.

Plans for rapid reaction against any insurgent move should be devised, involving counterinsurgent forces that can be ready at a moment's notice.

4. *Intelligence collection.* Whenever an organization is set up to collect intelligence, intelligence is bound to flow in, either because informers come spontaneously to the organization or because it goes after informers. The only real problem is how to prime the pump and hasten the flow.

Spontaneous information is hard to come by at this stage because of the population's fear of the insurgent and because of its lack of confidence in the counterinsurgent. To overcome this attitude, would-be informers should be given a safe, anonymous way to convey information. Many systems can be devised for the purpose, but the simplest one is to multiply opportunities for individual contacts between the population and the counterinsurgent personnel, every one of whom must participate in intelligence collection (not just the specialists). The census, the issuing of passes, the remuneration of workers, etc., are such opportunities.

When seeking informers, the counterinsurgent will have better results if he concentrates his efforts on those inhabitants who, by definition, ought to be his potential allies, i.e., those who would have least to win and most to lose through the insurgent's victory. The insurgent's program usually indicates who they may be.

If intelligence is still slow in coming, pressure may be applied. No citizen, even in a primitive country, can withstand for long the pressure from an uncooperative bureaucracy; insurgency conditions naturally increase the number of regulations that have to be complied with in daily life. Bureaucracy can be a powerful weapon in the hand of the counterinsurgent, provided it is used with moderation and restraint and never against a community as a whole but only against a few individuals.

In still tougher cases, visits to the inhabitants by pseudo insurgents are another way to get intelligence and to sow suspicion at the same time between the real guerrillas and the population.

5. *Starting to win the support of the population.* Implementing political reforms—if they have been conceived and announced by the government—would be premature at this stage. The time will be right when the insurgent political cells have been destroyed and when local leaders have emerged. In the political field, the task of the counterinsurgent leader is to discover what reforms are really wanted and to inform the higher echelons, or to determine whether the announced reforms conform with the popular wish.

On the other hand, the counterinsurgent can at once start working on various projects in the economic, social, cultural, and medical fields, where results are not entirely dependent on the active cooperation from the population. If these projects are deemed useful a priori for the population, they may even be imposed on it; the accusation of paternalism will soon be forgotten when results speak for themselves.

The counterinsurgent should also seize every opportunity to help the population with his own resources in personnel and equipment. Lack of ostentation is the best attitude, as his actions, good or bad, will always be commented upon and amplified by the public rumor.

In the field of information and psychological warfare, the problems and the tasks are numerous during this third step.

Propaganda Directed at the Counterinsurgent Forces

When forces are scattered among, and living with, the population, they need not be told any longer that they have to win its support. Being more vulnerable, they realize instinctively that their own safety depends on good relations with the local people. Good, friendly behavior will come about naturally on their part. The problem now is rather how to impress the counterinsurgent personnel with the necessity of remaining inwardly on guard while being outwardly friendly.

Another problem is how to make an active and efficient agent out of every member of the counterinsurgent forces, regardless of his rank and capacity. Where strict obedience to orders was sufficient in the preceding steps, initiative now becomes a must. Yet every individual effort must be channeled toward the same goal, deviations or honest mistakes kept to a minimum. This is the time when the local commander must assign specific tasks to his men every day, patiently brief them on their purposes, outline a way to fulfill them, anticipate the difficulties likely to arise, and propose a proper solution. After each particular operation, he must hold a meeting with his men, listen to their comments, draw the lessons, and spread the experience to other groups. If there is any way to teach initiative, this should do it.

Propaganda Directed at the Population

Three major goals are pursued during this step in regard to the population:

1. To get from it some measure of approval—or at least understanding—for the various actions taken by the counterinsurgent that affect the population (census, control of movements, imposition of tasks, etc.).
2. To lay the groundwork for the eventual dissociation of the population and the insurgent.
3. To prepare the commitment of sympathetic, but still neutral, elements.

The first point raises no great problem. It is just a matter of the counterinsurgent's telling the population what he proposes to do and why.

The difficulty comes with the other points. Propaganda, like terrorism, has an unfortunate tendency to backfire; of all the instruments of warfare, it is the most delicate, and its use requires caution, adherence to reality, and much advance planning. Yet if the target is a rural population, propaganda is most effective when its substance deals with local events, with problems with which the population is directly concerned, and when it is conducted on a person-to-person basis or addressed to specific groups (the men, the women, the youth, the elderly, etc.), rather than to the whole.

It is hardly possible to "precook" this sort of propaganda at a high level. One can easily see that the responsibilities placed upon the local commander are extremely heavy, especially when he has just begun to contact the population and has not yet assessed its reactions in a general way. How can he fulfill his role if the higher echelons do not come to his aid?

He should, at least, be relieved of any responsibility in the execution of the strategic-propaganda campaign, which should be the task of specialized mobile personnel. He should be assisted at all times by a deputy who can relieve him of most of the command routines. He should be provided with up-to-date guidelines for his tactical propaganda, conceived at the first- or second-higher echelon above him where authorities are still close enough to the local situation. He should also be reinforced by psychological-warfare personnel whenever necessary.

Propaganda Directed at the Insurgent

Among guerrillas, as among any human group, can be found a variety of thoughts, feelings, and degrees of commitment to the insurgent's cause. Treating them as a bloc would surely cement their solidarity. From now on, the goal of the counterinsurgent's psychological warfare should be, on the contrary, to divide their ranks, to stir up opposition between the mass and the leaders, to win over the dissidents.

This is a task that usually exceeds the possibilities of the local commander, for he has only an indirect channel of communication with the guerrillas—through the population—and the scattered guerrillas are usually roving over a territory larger than his own. Thus he can participate in, but not conduct, the campaign, which should be directed from a higher level.

THE FOURTH STEP: DESTRUCTION OF THE INSURGENT POLITICAL ORGANIZATION

The necessity for eradicating the insurgent political agents from the population is evident. The question is how to do it rapidly and efficiently, with a minimum of errors and bitterness.

This is, in essence, a police operation directed not against common criminals but against men whose motivations, even if the counterinsurgent disapproves of them, may be perfectly honorable. Furthermore, they do not participate directly, as a rule, in direct terrorism or guerrilla action and, technically, have no blood on their hands.

As these men are local people, with family ties and connections, and are hunted by outsiders, a certain feeling of solidarity and sympathy automatically exists toward them on the part of the population. Under the best circumstances, the police action cannot fail to have unpleasant aspects both for the population and for the counterinsurgent personnel living with it. This is why elimination of the agents must be achieved quickly and decisively.

But who can ever guarantee that mistakes will not be made and innocent people wrongly arrested? One of the insurgent's favorite tricks, indeed, is to mislead the counterinsurgent into arresting people who are hostile to the insurgency. Assuming that only the right men have been arrested, it would be dangerous and inefficient to let them be handled and interrogated by amateurs. All these reasons demand that the operation be conducted by professionals, by an organization that must in no way be confused with the counterinsurgent personnel working to win the support of the population. If the existing police cannot be trusted, then a special police force must be created for the purpose.

Whereas all the counterinsurgent personnel participates in intelligence acquisition, only the police should deal with the suspected agents. The police work, however, does not relieve the local counterinsurgent commander of his overall responsibility; the operation is conducted under his guidance and he must remain in constant liaison with the police during the "purge." When to purge is his decision, which should be based on two factors:

1. Whether enough intelligence is available to make the purge successful.
2. Whether the purge can be followed through.

In the red areas, the intelligence situation with regard to the insurgent political organization conforms usually to the following pattern. The boss and the top cell members are too heavily committed in the insurgency to be expected to change their attitude readily and to talk freely when arrested. Minor suspects, when arrested singly or in small groups, do not talk, either, because they fear that the subsequent counterinsurgent moves against the political agents would be traced to their disclosures. Yet every villager normally knows who the cell members are, or at least knows who is screening them. This suggests that an indirect approach could be easier and more certain than the direct one.

The procedure would be:

1. To arrest simultaneously a large group of minor suspects.
2. On the basis of their disclosures, to arrest the cell members.

There is, of course, a risk that the cell members, alerted by the first move, would vanish. The risk is small, however, for what could they do? If they join the guerrilla remnants, they would place an additional burden on them without substantially increasing their effectiveness, for a few more guerrillas do not change the situation much, while a political cell eliminated means a great change. If they move to another area where they would be outsiders, their value to the insurgent as agents would greatly decrease, and they would also be easily spotted and arrested. Thus, in the same way as expulsion of the guerrillas was a satisfactory result in the first step, the expulsion of the political agents is equally acceptable.

The moment to initiate the purge, then, is not when the cell members have been positively identified—a process that would take much time and leaves much to chance—but instead, when enough information has been gathered on a number of suspected villagers.

The operation would have little usefulness if the purged village were not now, or soon to be, occupied by counterinsurgent forces, for the guerrilla remnants would probably succeed in forcing a relatively unprotected population to create another cell, and the purge would have to be repeated all over again. The counterinsurgent should not hesitate to take risks in providing a detachment to occupy a purged village, but if he is absolutely unable to do so, it would be better to do nothing and wait for a better time.

The arrested cell members normally ought to be punished according to laws, since they have taken part in a conspiracy against the government. Nothing, however, is normal in a revolutionary war. If the counterinsurgent wishes to bring a quicker end to the war, he must discard some of the legal concepts that would be applicable to ordinary conditions. Automatic and rigid application of the law would flood the courts with minor and major cases, fill the jails and prison camps with people who could be won over, as well as with dangerous insurgents.

Leniency seems in this case a good practical policy, but not blind leniency. Although insurgent agents who repent sincerely can be released immediately, with no danger to the counterinsurgent's war effort, those who do not should be punished. Two criteria may serve to test their sincerity: a full confession of their past activity and a willingness to participate actively in the counterinsurgent's struggle. Another advantage of a policy of leniency is to facilitate the subsequent purges, for suspects who have previously seen arrested agents set free will be more inclined to talk.

The main concern of the counterinsurgent in his propaganda during this step is to minimize the possible adverse effects produced on the population by the arrests. He will have to explain frankly why it is necessary to destroy the insurgent political cells, and stress the policy of leniency to those who recognize their error. It does not matter if he is not believed, for the population's shock will be that much greater when the repentant agents are actually released.

THE FIFTH STEP: LOCAL ELECTIONS

Now begins the constructive part of the counterinsurgent program. What was done so far was to remove from the population the direct threat of the armed insurgents and the indirect threat of the political agents. Henceforth, the objective of the counterinsurgent's effort is to obtain the active support of the population, without which the insurgency cannot be liquidated.

The population's attitude immediately after the purge gives a fair indication of the difficulty of the task ahead. If the previous work was well conducted, the population should no longer have excuses for refusing its cooperation. The destruction of the political cells should normally bring about a sudden and dramatic change for the better in the climate; people will cease avoiding contact with counterinsurgent personnel and will no longer obey the various taboos ordered by the insurgent; the friendly elements will spontaneously come forward.

If the post-purge behavior remains what it was, it means:

1. That the purge was not complete, and this can easily be corrected.

2. That the population is not yet fully convinced of the counterinsurgent's will and ability to win, and reality will sooner or later overcome the people's reticence.

3. That the population is deeply and genuinely attached to the insurgent's cause. This is far more serious, for it shows the extent of the ideological handicap and how far the counterinsurgent must go in the way of reforms if he wants to win the support of the population. It does not mean, however, that the counterinsurgent is certain to lose the war, for he can still get (rather than win) the needed support. If his energy matches his unpopularity, he may wait until peace becomes the key issue, and he can rely to a greater extent on his own strength and on his small minority of supporters.

Whichever the case, the problem is to start organizing the participation of the population in the struggle. The way to do this is by placing local leaders in positions of responsibility and power.

Two opposite approaches may be considered. One is to designate men who have been previously identified as supporters, thus imposing them on the population. This should be a last-resort approach because the power and influence of these men will always be dependent on the counterinsurgent's strength. They will be regarded as puppets; the population will never feel any real responsibility toward them.

A better approach would be to call for absolutely free elections for local provisional self-government, thus letting leaders emerge naturally from the population, which will feel more bound to them since they are the product of its choice. The danger that neutrals or even undetected insurgent supporters could be elected is small because the population will realize that the counterinsurgent knows by now who was for whom, especially if he has spread the rumor that this was part of the information he sought for from the arrested agents. Chances are that the population will elect people known or suspected to be counterinsurgent supporters.

There is a far greater danger that the population will elect not natural leaders but men chosen for their presumed ability to placate the counterinsurgent. An obvious sign of this would be the absence of young men among the local leaders elected.

Whatever the results of the elections, the counterinsurgent must accept them with the publicly announced proviso that these new local leaders are temporarily in office until definitive elections when peace has been restored all over the country.

The propaganda directed toward the population during this step should stress four points: the importance of the elections, complete freedom for the voters, the necessity of voting, and the provisional nature of the elected local government.

THE SIXTH STEP: TESTING THE LOCAL LEADERS

The ultimate results of the counterinsurgent's efforts in regard to the population depend on the effectiveness of the men who have just been elected. If they are worthless, the counterinsurgent will have to count only on himself; he will thus remain an outsider vis-à-vis the population and be unable to reduce substantially his strength in the selected area in order to apply it elsewhere.

The first thing to do, therefore, is to test these new local leaders. The principle of the test is simple: They are given concrete tasks and they are judged on their ability to fulfill them. There are, at this stage, any number of tasks that can be assigned: running the local government, undertaking local projects in the social and economic fields, taking over some police functions, levying volunteers for self-defense units, propagandizing, etc.

The counterinsurgent will soon find which leaders are living up to expectations. His action will tend to consolidate their position and to build them up, using for this purpose all the available assets and the power of the counterinsurgent regime. As for those who failed in the test, his action will tend to eliminate or to shunt them away with the support, or at least the consent, of the population.

It may happen in a few local elections that the men elected are all worthless, and no better candidates are available. This would be plainly a case of bad luck, against which little can be done on the local scale except gerrymandering the constituency to merge it with a neighboring one where better men are available. This problem is less serious when it is a matter of discovering hundreds of local leaders than when it involves finding the best counterinsurgent leader on a national scale.

The various tasks entrusted to the local leaders have, of course, more than a test value. Most are also designed to win the support of the population through these leaders. Some tasks are conceived to make the population take an active part in the struggle against the insurgent: organizing selfdefense units, recruiting full-time auxiliaries for the regular forces, organizing intelligence and control nets and propaganda teams.

Three of the many problems confronting the counterinsurgent during this step require particular attention.

The elected leaders are conspicuous targets for the insurgent and they should be protected, yet not in such a way that they rely entirely on the counterinsurgent's protection. They should be told, on the contrary, that the support of the population is their best protection and it is up to them to get it.

A certain degree of paternalism cannot be avoided initially since the elected leaders are both unknown and untrained, but a paternalistic attitude on the part of the counterinsurgent is self-defeating, for it will promote only passive yes-men, a plague in counterinsurgency situations. Paternalism must, therefore, be discarded as soon as possible, even if this involves risks.

The tasks to be done require logistical support in the form of funds, equipment, and qualified personnel. These should be made readily available and given with a minimum of red tape. Moreover, the manipulation of this logistical support is a political act, and it must be allocated with a priority in favor of villages or districts where the population is most active on the side of the counterinsurgent. A weapon that has such a stimulating value must not be utilized indiscriminately.

When in a part of the selected area, the situation has reached the stage where the population actively helps the counterinsurgent, it means that a breakthrough has been achieved, and it should be exploited at once to influence the less-advanced sectors. To do so is the main goal of the propaganda during this step.

As propaganda is much more convincing when it emanates from the population instead of coming from the counterinsurgent personnel, local inhabitants should be persuaded to act as propagandists not only in their own area but outside. When they do so, the war is virtually won in the selected area.

Another certain sign that a breakthrough has occurred is when spontaneous intelligence increases sharply.

THE SEVENTH STEP: ORGANIZING A PARTY

As the work proceeds in the area, tested leaders will finally appear in each village and town. They will eventually have to be grouped and organized within a national counterinsurgent political party. There are several reasons for this:

1. A party is the instrument of politics, particularly in revolutionary war where politics counts for so much. The best policy may be worthless for the counterinsurgent so long as he does not possess the necessary instrument to implement it.

2. The newly found leaders who emerged locally operate within their own local sphere, isolated from their neighbors. They are able at best to oppose local resistance to the insurgent who, on his part, is organized not only on the local but also on the national scale, with all the intermediate levels. Thus, the insurgent retains a considerable political advantage, which cannot be tolerated.

3. The new leaders' powers over the population are mostly of an administrative nature. If their leadership has to extend to the political field, it can do so only through a party.

4. Their links with the population are based on a single, official ballot. They are fragile as long as the leaders are not backed by a political machine solidly rooted in the population. Just as the counterinsurgent himself has worked to discover the leaders, these must in turn find militants among the population; to keep the militants together, the leaders need the framework, the support, and the guidance of a political party.

Is it best to group the local leaders and the militants within an existing party or to create a new one? The answer depends obviously on the particular circumstances, the prestige of the existing party, the quality of its leadership, and the appeal of its platform.

The creation of a new party raises the problem of its political program. It cannot be undertaken as long as the counterinsurgent has not decided what political reforms he intends to accomplish.

Although in peacetime most political parties—with the notable exception of the Communists—aim at expanding their membership with little or no regard to the candidates' aptitudes, insurgency conditions impose more caution. The counterinsurgent political party should select its members carefully, and rely more on quality than on quantity.

The creation of a party is neither an easy nor a quick undertaking. The fact remains, nevertheless, that the local leaders have to be grouped in some kind of national organization as soon as a sufficient number of them has emerged. At the beginning, regional associations can serve temporarily for the purpose.

THE EIGHTH STEP: WINNING OVER OR SUPPRESSING THE LAST GUERRILLAS

The counterinsurgent, while concentrating on the tasks necessary for winning the support of the population, has not neglected to continue tracking the guerrillas left in the selected area after the intensive operations described in the first step. He may even have liquidated them completely. If not, he still has to finish with the last remnants.

The tactical problem results from their dilution; from their feeble offensive activity; from their avoidance of contact with the population, which dries up sources of intelligence; in some cases, from terrain difficulties. Under these conditions, hunting the guerrillas with the usual ambushes, patrols, and small-scale operations could be time-consuming and not very productive. This is why it would be more profitable for the counterinsurgent to revert now to the same massive military effort that characterized the first step, but this time with the important added asset of the population participating effectively in the operations.

The main difficulty is a psychological one and it originates in the counterinsurgent's own camp. Responsible people will question why it is necessary to make such an effort at this stage, when everything seems to be going so well. Arguments are not lacking against this line of reasoning. The fact is that guerrillas who still roam the area are certain to be a hard core, a breed produced by natural selection, and they can hardly be left behind for the population and a skeleton garrison to cope with. Thorough final operations will show the counterinsurgent's determination to smash his opponent and should bring valuable political benefits both within and without the selected area, on the population, on the insurgents, and on the counterinsurgent's own forces.

The basic operational principle to eliminate guerrillas who are few in number and isolated from the population is to force them to move, to become "roving bandits," and to catch them as they attempt to cross successive nets of counterinsurgent forces. Such were, in essence, the tactics followed with great success by the Chinese Communists themselves in south China in 1950–52, when they liquidated the Nationalist remnants.

The troops' requirement are great, but since the guerrillas are operating in very small groups of a few men each, and are feebly armed besides, the net may be entrusted to the population which is temporarily mobilized and armed, and led by professional cadres drawn from the static units. Mobile reserves assigned to the area for the occasion will be used to flush out the guerrillas.

How long this effort can or should be maintained is a matter of local circumstances, the main factor being the disruption of the population's life. The best time, obviously, is when farming is at a standstill.

The military efforts need to be supplemented by an intensive psychological offensive against the guerrillas; the trump card here is an amnesty offer. This presents some danger but less than at any other time because the counterinsurgent has reached now a real position of strength in the selected area, based on the effective support of the population.

Even such a large effort, however, cannot be expected to bring a complete end to the insurgency in the area; a few guerrillas will still manage to survive. It may be interesting to note in this respect that in September, 1962, fourteen years after the start of the insurgency in Malaya, 20 to 30 Communist guerrillas were still holding out in the deep jungle inside Malaya, not counting 300 more operating on the Malaya-Thailand border.

These survivors may give up one day if the insurgency collapses, or they may leave the area for good, or they may hold out. In this last case, they should no longer be a problem.

CONCLUDING REMARKS

Such is, in the author's view, the basic mechanism of counterinsurgency warfare. Whether in the cold or in the hot revolutionary war, its essence can be summed up in a single sentence: Build (or rebuild) a political machine from the population upward. The idea is simple. How difficult it may be to implement it can be gathered from the following observations, written in a context utterly alien to revolutionary situation, in a peaceful and well-developed country, and precisely for this reason the more relevant to our problem:

> Public indifference to politics is disheartening. On that snowy February morning when I started ringing doorbells, the first four families visited said bluntly, "We never vote." In my congressional district there are about 334,000 adults eligible to vote, but of these, 92,000 do not even bother to register. Of the 334,000 only 217,000 voted in the Kennedy-Nixon election.
>
> A recent study at the University of Michigan shows that of 100 registered adults, only seven attend political meetings of any kind, only four have ever given money to a campaign, only three have ever worked for a candidate and only two actually serve as working members of any political party.
>
> The burden of ruling our nation falls on the shoulders of an appallingly small number of people. As I campaign, month after month, I see these same people again and again. The others I never touch.[1]

Napoleon remarked that "War is a simple art, all a matter of execution."

What would happen, the reader may ask, if the party created by the counterinsurgent eventually adopts the original insurgent's program? A simple answer is, that would be a different story. The Allies won the war in 1918, "the war to end all wars." What they did with their victory is another story. There are no final solutions in human affairs. The risk that a specially created counterinsurgent party may later espouse the very cause of the insurgent does indeed exist, particularly when the insurgency was based essentially on ethnic or national differences, as, for instance, in the current conflict between the Kurds and Iraqis. If this happens, all the counterinsurgent has really won is a respite, which is in itself a precious commodity. He can hope that the leaders of the new party, instead of embarking on a new insurgency, will choose to follow a more peaceful path. He can concede to them reforms he was forced to refuse to an intransigent insurgent party born out of terror and violence. Is this not, in fact, what occurred in Malaya where the British granted to others what they had refused to the Communist insurgents? As long as the revolutionary situation exists, even in a dormant form, as long as the problem that gave rise to the insurgency has not been eliminated, the danger persists and will require a variable degree of vigilance from the counterinsurgent.

Is it always possible to defeat an insurgency? This work, through a common intellectual accident, may have given the impression that the answer is a strong affirmative. When one learns in military schools about the offensive, one gets the impression that nothing can resist a well-mounted attack, which appears as the "irresistible force." Then one learns about the defensive and gets the impression that nothing can break through a well-conceived defense, "the immovable mass." (Let us disregard the nuclear-armed missile against which no defense has yet been devised.)

Obviously, it is not always possible to defeat an insurgency. The Greek insurgency was doomed from the start. So was the French counterinsurgency in Indochina. Except for these clear cases, victory in most of the other recent revolutionary wars could possibly have gone to either camp. The outcome was not decided in advance for Mao Tse-tung or for Chiang Kai-shek, for Batista or for Castro, for the FLN or for the French in Algeria.

Insurgencies in the recent past have stemmed from two major causes: (1) the rise of nationalism in colonial territories, and (2) Communist pressure, the latter sometimes inspiring and directing the insurgency alone, sometimes combining with the former, but always present and active.

Colonialism is dead now except for a few isolated instances against which the "wind of change" concentrates with fury. One would expect the issue to die with it. Unfortunately, this has not happened, for after colonialism comes "neocolonialism," which is not merely a Communist slogan. There are no colonies in Latin America apart from the Guianas, British Honduras, and other insignificant places. Yet the whole continent is seething with unrest. The revolutionary war in Cuba—which was not a colony—was but a sign. "As things are going now, the greatest outburst in history is brewing in Latin America," warned Eduardo Santos, the former President of Colombia.[2] The issue of neocolonialism is not confined to Latin America. Sincere and not so sincere complaints against economic exploitation by the West can also be heard in Africa and Asia. Few among the newly emancipated nations have been able to recover from the inevitable disorders that, even under the best circumstances, have marked the departure of the former rulers. Fewer still have been able to demonstrate that independence meant immediate progress for the masses, as they were led to believe. It would be a miracle if the perils and difficulties of the transition from colonial to national rule, actively fanned by the Communists, failed to result in scattered unrest, uprisings—and insurgencies.

There is no evidence that Communist pressure has abated, that the Communist apparatus for spreading revolution has been dismantled. Soviet Russia's line may change now, but it may switch again, as it has in the past, before Stalin, under Stalin, and after Stalin. Whatever the latest Soviet stand, Red China clearly intends to capitalize on her chief asset, to continue exporting her chief product—a coherent doctrine for revolution in "colonial and semicolonial countries where similar conditions prevail," as Liu Shao-ch'i said. She claimed leadership over these countries as early as 1951. On July 1 of that year, when the Chinese Communist Party celebrated its thirtieth anniversary, all the major speeches made on that occasion insisted on the world-wide importance of the Chinese Revolution. One of the orators in Peking, Lu Ting-yi, then head of the propaganda department of the Central Committee, said explicitly:

The prototype of the revolution in capitalist countries is the October Revolution.

The prototype of the revolution in colonial and semicolonial countries is the Chinese Revolution, the experience of which is invaluable for the people of these countries.

An ideological map of the world (see Figure 4), also issued in 1951 in China, translates vividly the implications of this new, if perhaps unilateral, version of the Treaty of Tordesillas, by which Pope Alexander VI in 1494 gave Spain all lands discovered more than 370 leagues west of the Cape Verde Islands, and Portugal the right to explore and annex all lands in Africa and east of the Spanish sphere. In this 1951 map, Canada and Australia were rigidly considered by the Chinese as colonial countries, Latin America and Japan as capitalist territories. Subsequent statements by Chinese Communists indicate that all Latin America and Japan—this last an "American semicolony"—are within the Chinese sphere of influence, while Australia and Canada fall within the Soviet sphere. (See Figure 5.)

Figure 4.   Ideological Map of the World as Seen by the Chinese Communists in 1951

Figure 5.   Ideological Map of the World as Revised According to Subsequent Chinese Communist Statements

The world is thus divided neatly into three major blocs, roughly equal in size and population, if not in stage of economic development:

The friends, the "sister countries," i.e., the Communist states.

The potential allies, i.e., the "colonial and semicolonial" countries.

The enemy, i.e., the "capitalist" countries.

Hence, the Chinese Communist strategy, the principle of which—if not the leadership role of China—seems to have been accepted by Soviet

Russia: As a first step, deny the colonial bloc to the capitalists; as a second step, grab control of it. Then the Communists will have a two-to-one superiority over the capitalists in area and population; by the mere closing of markets and disruption of trade channels, they can hope to bring the capitalists to their knees, at minimum risk, progressively. The Communist military strength will serve to protect revolutionary gains and to deter or overcome any last-minute reaction to this strategy on the part of the capitalists.

How the advent of nuclear weapons and the danger of accidental collision or how the current Sino-Soviet dispute has affected the chances for success of this strategy can be endlessly argued. The fact remains, nevertheless, that even if the Russian bear is turning suddenly into a horse—strong but peaceful—the Chinese, whose determination can leave no doubt in the mind of those who have watched how they operate on their own territory, are certain to keep plugging their line and thus to attract extremists, the very people who usually spark insurgencies.

There is, finally, a further reason to assume that the list of revolutionary wars is not closed. It is certainly easier to launch an insurgency than to repress it. We have seen how much disorder the Greek Communists were able to occasion, even though the essential prerequisites for their success were not met. With so many successful insurgencies in the recent years, the temptation will always be great for a discontented group, anywhere, to start the operations. They may gamble on the inherent weakness of the counterinsurgent (inherent because of the asymmetry between one camp and the other), they may gamble on support from one side of the world or the other. Above all, they may gamble on the effectiveness of an insurgency-warfare doctrine so easy to grasp, so widely disseminated today that almost anybody can enter the business.

It is safe to assume that the West, almost automatically, will be involved directly or indirectly in the coming revolutionary wars. With the Communists pulling one way, chances are that the West will probably be involved on the side of order, i.e., on the side of the counterinsurgent.

That is why this book has been written.

Cambridge, Mass.
October, 1963

NOTES

1. James A. Michener. "What Every New Candidate Should Know," *The New York Times Magazine,* September 23, 1962.

2. As quoted in William Benton, "The Voice of Latin America," in *Britannica Book of the Year, 1961.*

INDEX

ABOUT THE AUTHOR

DAVID GALULA (1919-1967) was born to French parents in Tunisia and raised in Morocco, earning his baccalauréat in Casablanca and attending the military academy at Saint-Cyr. Graduated on the eve of World War II, he saw action in North Africa, Italy, and France. An officer of the marine infantry in the old colonial army, he was assigned to China and also served with the United Nations as a military observer in Greece and military attaché in Hong Kong. Colonel Galula was stationed in Algeria at the time of the revolt by the French army. Shortly before retiring he wrote *Counterinsurgency Warfare: Theory and Practice*, while in residence at the Center for International Affairs, Harvard University.